LITERATURE IN ITS PLACE

Literature in its Place

James Britton

Boynton/Cook
HEINEMANN
Portsmouth NH

Boynton/Cook Publishers
A Subsidiary of
Heinemann Educational Books, Inc.
361 Hanover Street
Portsmouth, NH 03801

First published 1993

Library of Congress Cataloging-in-Publication Data

Britton, James N.
   Literature in its place / James Britton.
      p. cm.
   Includes bibliographical references.
   ISBN 0-86709-315-3
   1. English literature—Study and teaching. 2. English literature—History and criticism—Theory, etc. 3. Literature—Philosophy.
4. Language arts. 5. Imagination. I. Title.
PR33.B69 1992
820.71'2—dc20   92-24089
                                                                      CIP

Cover design by Twyla Bogaard
Printed in the United States of America
92 93 94 95 96   10 9 8 7 6 5 4 3 2 1

CONTENTS

To
Roberta
in
loving memory

Introduction

To suppose that imagination is in itself a gift granted only to the privileged few is a sad mistake, yet it is a view that many responsible people have held. There have always been teachers who expect little in the way of surprises from children they believe to be lacking in imagination—though the myth of the unimaginative child offers a good deal less as a credible excuse than it did, say, fifty years ago. The established adult writer may well be more skeptical on this matter: I have been surprised at the way some writers claim special abilities not given to Tom, Dick, and Harry, abilities that they are unwilling to look for in the imaginative utterances of children. What we have striven to do, for many years now, is to open the way to see the stories that children tell, the scenes they enact, the songs they sing, as early steps in a continuous progress that runs unbroken from child's play to the images that poets and novelists use in reflecting upon the human predicament

John Stuart Mill gave us a philosopher's definition of the imagination in these words: "that which enables us, by a voluntary effort, to conceive the absent as if it were present, the imaginary as if it were real, and to clothe it in the feelings which, if it were indeed real, it would bring along with it." And he glosses that as "the power by which one human being enters into the mind and circumstances of another" (1950, p. 60-62).

Seen in such severely logical terms, I don't think anyone could doubt that imagination is an essential element in the powers of perception and cerebration that characterize human mentality, and not a special gift bestowed only on writers, painters, and other artists. And then, like so many of our abilities, we have to admit that it grows above all from use—from use in ever wider and more complicated areas of our concern.

Let me illustrate what seems to be the difference between youngsters whose imaginative capacities have been sharpened by use and others in whom they have not. This was reported to me some years ago by Joan, a student training to be a teacher. She had spent the summer vacation working in a factory near her home where many of the employees had been her school friends. Thus she was on friendly terms with the regular workers, and when one of the girls reported to her that she had had a great row with her boyfriend on the previous evening, it was evident that she was very upset. She seemed to have lost all hope. Joan believed that this was a failure of the imagination, a failure to suppose that tomorrow might be different, that next week might bring a reconciliation, or that some other affair might turn up, or at best that there might be more fish in the sea than the one she thought she had on her line. Of course, we may from time to time suffer a disappointment or a loss too grievous to be borne—but this did not appear to be in that category.

Starting from what was probably a common background, one of the two friends, Joan, had developed her imagination through her dealings with stories—perhaps acting them out, perhaps telling them, but certainly reading and discussing them. To achieve this is to experience the educational effect of literature in its essential and socially mediated form. For stories, accounts of experience by ourselves, or other people, real or imagined, are part of the conviviality of many social occasions. And the power of the imagination may be operating as little more than an aspect of self-concern where that growth has not been fostered.

To risk a generalization, societies moved out of more primitive organization when they determined to establish schools—places where their immature members would meet together to learn about the physical and social environment in which they found themselves, and about how it came to be that way. I think we are so accustomed to think of learning in the context of schooling that we may forget examples of earlier modes by which we have continued from an early age to learn—from stories and from the verbal and dramatic arts in general.

"Culture" is not an easy term to apply because it is used to mean such diverse phenomena. Here is a use that seems to me appropriate to the purposes this book attempts to explore. Donald Winnicott, pediatrician and psychoanalyst, speaks of play as the first manifestation of "cultural experience." But he finds it difficult to define culture itself: "The accent is on experience. In using the word culture I am thinking of the inherited tradition. I am thinking of something that is in the common pool of humanity, into which individuals and groups of people may contribute, and from which we may all draw *if we have somewhere to put what we find*" (1971, pp. 102–3).

Bearing in mind that the individuals pursue interests of many kinds—practical, scientific, political—it seems right to speak also of a common pool of value judgments, of the verdicts that underlie the human condition—and to see that we profit from that, provided we can pay the entrance fee—that is to say, if experience already ours provides a context in which the cultural belief makes sense.

The common pool of humanity is not, it seems to me, a source of naked information, information offered without evaluation. The making of value judgments is a work of the imagination, appreciating what the environment, physical and social, may offer us and conceiving alternative possibilities, drawing upon the common pool of humanity. It is a mode of learning that went on long before there were schools and takes place today in families, and social groups, as well as in schools.

This book is concerned with the verbal arts—whether in contemplation, in speech, or in writing. In whatever mode, it is a culture-learning process, and what is learnt may be drawn from "the common pool of humanity."

Acknowledgments

I am grateful to a number of people who have read and commented on early drafts of chapters of this book, as follows: Myra Barrs, Penny Blackie, Alison Britton, Tony Burgess, Martin Lightfoot, Nancy Martin, Jane Miller, Margaret Spencer (England); Merron Chorny, Joan Green, Donald Rutledge (Canada); Mary Barr, Betty Bailey, Bob Boynton, Dixie Goswami, Mary K. Healy, Judith Langley, Gordon Pradl, Geoffrey Summerfield (U.S.A.)

Chapter One

The Anatomy of Human Experience
The Role of Inner Speech

Waking in the morning, throwing back the bedclothes, already assailed by an unfocused sense of the day's responsibilities; parting the curtains and looking up at the sky—to approve or disapprove. Emerging into the silent house, moving in a way that will preserve its silence as a kind of freedom, yet at the same time submitting to the routine activities that respond to the needs and expectations of others—the acts of an automaton fulfilling inbuilt neuromuscular instructions. But look far enough into the past and it will be clear that the patterns were probably first recognized in other people and imitated—clumsily perhaps, playfully perhaps, certainly with deliberation. Experience grows for me as I take over these discovered behaviors, adapted to my biological self and the social environment in which I operate.

"Recognizing," "discovering," "observing"—these indicate too passive a process for what appears in fact to take place. If we begin at the earliest stages of infancy, the active world starts to impinge on the infant as a kind of invitation to miming. Routines or formats of interactive behavior which are instituted by an adult (most often the mother), by becoming recognizable—that is to say "familiar"— emerge as distinct from the meaningless flux of other, unfamiliar events. They are likely to be accompanied by talk on the mother's part—talk that puts into words the activities she initiates, but at the

1

same time embeds them in a more general, if fragmentary, representation of the life of the family. While the infant at this stage can respond only to the emotional intonations of the talk and not to its encoded meanings, it will not be long before such talk begins to fulfill the crucial role of providing her/him with the key to linguistic meaning. What had become meaningful from enacted routines may then be matched with what is communicated by the mother's verbal behavior; and we must assume that it is that matching process that leads to a gradual mastery of the spoken language. Thereafter, talk becomes a principal means of interacting with other people, and it is this continued interaction that constitutes the recognition/production of meaningful behavior.

So the interacting, responding, observing provide the indispensable key to the origins of those patterns of behavior and then to their subsequent modification on my part as they constitute my accumulating experience. And on this aforementioned morning, glancing at the weather, contemplating the day's activities, interacting with members of the household, making some demands and responding to the demands of others, it is still the alert and sensitive interacting that holds the key. Should that become something I am no longer capable of, I might as well go back to bed and stay there!

If I were to complete a detailed account of the morning's activities—describing the food and the utensils, the drink and the layout of the table—I should be likely to create an increasing certainty that my home belonged to a particular geographical and social area. There might, of course, be anomalies—reflections of activities observed and imitated during periods of my life when I lived in other surroundings, foreign countries, perhaps, or came under alien influences. Patterns of behavior will distinguish not only my individual self but also my family, and beyond that my social groups—local, regional, national.

A closer look at adult/child interaction will make quite clear how important is the role played by exchange of talk. Here is a brief interaction between Laurie, my grandchild, at three years eight months, and myself. She is paying a visit to our home and we are in the garden, talking, about a thrushes' nest, now empty.

Laurie: Where's the birds' nest?

Me: It's still there, Darling, but . . . they're not . . .

L: Are the birds coming?

M: No, they're not coming, darling because . . .

L: Why?

M: Because they've left the nest.

L: When will they be little babies?

M: They were little babies—they're not now—they're big birds now.

L: When were they little babies?

M: Oh, about six months ago.

L: 's a long while ago.

M: Yes.

L: And I was BIG!

M: Were you?

L: Yes—big.

M: How big were you?

L: Not like Mummy and Daddy.

M: Mm?

L: Not like Mummy and Daddy . . . (a distraction) Fluff!

M: That's fluff from the tree—that's seeds that fall down from that tree. Do you see where it's coming down? . . . Do you see that coming down? That's where all that comes from.

L: How are they coming down here?

M: Well . . . that's . . . see, lots of it—some more there—everywhere there's fluff—come down from that tree—that's called a . . . an aspen.

L: Why is no more birds going in there—in the nest?

M: Eh, I don't know, love—I think—they've gone somewhere else, perhaps.

L: Why are they leaving all the nest there?

M: Well, praps they'll come back to it next year when the birds have another family—praps they'll come back.

L: Why?

M: Well, they built it there, didn't they?

(Other members of the family arrive on the scene and the conversation is over.)

It will certainly not be true of all children everywhere, but with a great many of the children I have known, or learned of from records, by far the greater number of exploratory, interactive meaning-making occasions have been in the context of make-believe rather than in daily real-life activities. In cooperative make-believe the child is likely to be the one who calls up the scene and directs the action; and in doing so, Vygotsky points out, "the child learns to act in a cognitive, rather than an externally visual realm, by relying on internal tendencies and motives and not on incentives supplied by external things" (1978, p. 96). In this way the number and variety of activated concerns is vastly increased, but—even more significant—these concerns are inherently representative of the child's state of experience. There is no shortage of recordings to illustrate this aspect of interaction: here Laurie and I take part in a game of shops earlier on the same day as the garden encounter recorded above. In one form or another, playing shops had become a favorite make-believe scenario with the three-and-a-half-year-old:

(A shop space is marked out by a tea-trolley [a pretend cooking stove] and a gate-legged coffeetable.)

Laurie: Switch. I turn 'em all on—they're cooking—switch What cake do you like?

Me: Have you got chocolate cake? I like chocolate cake.

L: Yes . . . Why does this fall over? It's . . . Why does this tip over—this one doesn't tip over—it's got wheels! Why? (The coffee table versus the tea-trolley) Look there. Are you coming? There! I turn the cakes off: they're READY!

M: Oh, good—are they cooked?

L: I'm going to pass these—I'm walking did you see—Come here! Come in my shop and I'll give you one. What kind?

M: I'd like chocolate cake please.

L: O.K. How much money?

M: Two shillings—twenty pence—twenty pence.

L: Here 'tis then.

M: Do I give it to you, then? O.K. There's twenty pence for the cake . . . What's that cake?

L: A shallow cake?

M: Yes.

L: A brown one or a yellow one or a pink one.

M: Chocolate—a brown one. Do you say these are shallow cakes—do you call them? What are these then?

L: Those are chocolate cakes with banana.

M: Oh, that sounds lovely. How much are they?

L: Fifty pence.

M: How much?

L: These will be . . .

M: Fifteen pence?

L: Thank you.

M: Thank you . . . Lovely. What kind of cakes are those?

L: China cakes.

M: Chung cakes..? What's the word,

L: Chi-i-i-ina cakes.

M: China cakes—oh—I'll have one of those.

L: *[abashed]* Well—there are only these many. *Please can you go to another shop?*

M: Oh—yea—O.K. O.K,

L: Ask Alison for one.

M: Bye-bye, thank you.

L: Bye!

Spoken dialogue is at this stage the principal means by which a child's linguistic resources are recruited and experiences internalized. Some children will, as early as this, attempt spoken monologue, but when they do their utterances are likely to be of the somewhat dream-like, loose, illogical kind that I have called *spiels* (1972, p. 83)—word-spinning performances, jigsaw collections of remembered phrases—offered as entertainment to admiring listeners, not as conversation. Utterances as celebration would designate some of these performances, as for example the following spoken in a sing-song voice by my daughter Clare at three years zero months:

> Angels at head, fairies at foot
> The stars are shining with golden light
> Hit on the ball with golden light
> Loo-ing, loo-ing. Darling child
> The children in bed
> *—it's the big one that's saying it, you see—*
> Lighting up the candles so early
> Holy night—silent night.

I should add that the sources of the language of most *spiels* would be more diverse and less easily recognized than those of this example.

Genuine monologic speech is another matter—and a later development, though as might be expected, the transition may not be at all clearly marked. That is to say, expressive, performance-directed speech may play some part in utterances that would otherwise be recognized as communicative monologue carrying cognitive messages.

The transition from dialogic to monologic speech in young children has been helpfully described by A. R. Luria (1981). He traced the development of a child's problem-solving speech from its beginnings as expanded—fully verbalized—vocal speech through speech for oneself, where it becomes abbreviated in the process of being internalized—becoming, that is to say, inner speech.

> Only when external speech has become abbreviated and converted into inner speech does it become possible to carry out the opposite process, i.e., the expansion of this inner speech into an external,

connected text with its characteristic semantic coherence . . . . We would argue that once a child has mastered these operational components of expanded speech, he/she goes through an equally complex path to develop real speech activity. This activity is guided by a motive, is subject to a specific goal, and constitutes a constantly regulated, closed semantic system. (p. 158)

These are developments that he would have expected to occur as a child approaches school age and the earliest monologues, he suggested, are likely to take a narrative form.

An early example of what I take to be essentially monologic speech is provided by Laurie at four years one month in a make-believe situation in which she is the mother and I play the part of her small child. The situation she implies is fictional (she has in reality only one younger sister), although it clearly represents some aspects of her own real experience. The tape recording shows hesitations that suggest she is improvising as she speaks—that is to say, in Luria's terms, that her utterance is an expanded version of her inner speech. I think it is a fair description to call the piece as a whole *enacted* (rather than related) *narrative*. Finally, if we accept Vygotsky's (1978, p. 102) view that in make-believe play a young child is able to act some months—or even years—ahead of his/her chronological age, it may well be that true monologue is likely, in the case of many children, to make its earliest appearance in make-believe play.

Laurie: Now it's time for little darlings to go to sleep.

Me: Yes.

L: You've got to go to sleep now. Your blanket—pillow. Lie down! Now you're going to have a little—if you don't want to go to sleep—you *must* go to sleep, 'cos—or you will be afraid of night,'cos *the owls* come at night . . . . Yes, they go to-whoo! They don't frighten *you*—they don't eat you, only rats or mice— that's good, isn't it?

M: Yes.

L: Now I've got to sort your cover, 'cos you messed it up last night, didn't you?

M: Yes, I wriggled about so much, didn't I?

L: Yes, 'cos you're afraid of the *owl*, aren't you.

M: Yes.

L: Tonight I have to sleep in my own room which is downstairs and Dad sleeps downstairs too and you only sleep *up*stairs. And the baby *sleeps* (pause) downstairs too and the big girls—and your two sisters sleep down too and you only sleep up, don't you? So you have to be very quiet. If you hear—if you—um—hear a *monster*, I'll come running up. I hope—if you dream about

one, just cry and come down and say "Oo-oo, Mummy, I had a bad dream."
Yes. Now you're going to go to sleep, aren't you? Close your eyes!

It seems to me that the play of imagination illustrated in tran-
scripts of this kind provides a key to the continuing role of creative
language in human existence—whether manifested in the verbal
arts or in the probing curiosity that empowers scientific inquiry.
Vygotsky has spelled out his account of the transition from make-believe behavior to the birth of the imagination:

> Imagination is a new psychological process for the child; it is not
> present in the consciousness of the very young child, is totally
> absent in animals, and represents a specifically human form of
> conscious activity. Like all functions of consciousness, it originally
> arises from action. The old adage that child's play is imagination in
> action must be reversed: we can say that imagination in adolescents
> and school children is play without action (1978, p. 93)

It will raise no eyebrows to acknowledge here the existence of a
close developmental link between make-believe play in infancy and
the practice of the arts at all stages from kindergarten to the grave.
The link has been widely and variously formulated. In *Play, Dreams
and Imitation* for example, Piaget (1951) characterizes make-believe
as *symbolic assimilation* and concludes that it is "reintegrated in
thought in the form of creative imagination" or "spontaneous constructive activity" (p. 155). Freud (see Vygotsky, 1971, p. 73) claims
that "the poet does the same things as the child at play: he creates
a world, which he takes very seriously, with a lot of enthusiasm and
animation, and at the same time very sharply sets it apart from
reality." Vygotsky goes on to state his own view that art functions for
the child in ways that differ from its role for an adult, and he explains
this by referring to the work of Chukovsky (1963) on the young child's
use of nursery rhymes: the way their topsy-turvy nonsense appeals
to a child at a time when he is consolidating his mastery of the
actual. "By dragging a child into a topsy-turvy world," Vygotsky
writes, "we help his intellect work, because the child becomes interested in creating such a topsy-turvy world for himself in order to
become more effectively the master of the laws governing the real
world" (1971, p. 258). If rhymes and stories—seen as works of literature—have this effect, they will clearly be serving a purpose that
diminishes as the child grows older has what T. S. Eliot—in his poem
Animula—called "the imperatives of is and seems" grow less insis-
tent. Vygotsky goes on to suggest that while adults have no such
predominance of "seems" over "is" to contend with, there is also for
them in art something of the same dualism—that art serves to
present modified, even somewhat distorted, views of reality, and thus

has the effect of strengthening in the viewer his/her grasp of the nature of reality, while at the same time, let me add, exploring the structures of *what it might become*. In short, art by this view is "a method for building life."

It is an interesting feature of Vygotsky's book that while it bears the title *The Psychology of Art*, its subject matter—its exemplification throughout—is, in one form or another, *literature*, the verbal arts.

It is my purpose in the rest of this chapter to ask how central a function in human development is the use of language in creative, constructive modes—how important to us, in other words, are social products of a literary nature and what do we achieve by experimenting in the production of such works? In pursuing this inquiry, there are two ideas put forward by early Soviet students of language—contemporaries and probably professional associates of Vygotsky—that we need to consider at this stage:

1. The notion that meaning is, in the first instance, interpersonal, constantly created, adapted, modified in the course of person-to-person verbal exchange. (The same idea has been elegantly put by Georges Gusdorf, the French philosopher [1965, p. 48]; "In essence, language is not of one but of many; it is *between*. It expresses the relational being of man. . . . The self does not by itself alone have to carve out for itself an access to being—because the self exists only in reciprocity with the other. An isolated self can truly be said to be only an abstraction.")

2. The idea that human experience in its organized and recoverable form is a network of verbal meanings. Volosinov (1973) spells out this view in the course of answering the question, "How, in fact, is another's speech received?"

   Everything vital to the evaluative reception of another's utterance, everything of ideological value, is expressed in the material of inner speech. After all, it is not a mute, wordless creature that receives such an utterance, but a human being full of inner words. All his experiences. . . . exist encoded in his inner speech, and only to that extent to they come into contact with speech received from outside. Word comes into contact with word. (p. 118)

However, it does seem to me that the encoding process is a selective one, and that the selection will entail an element of individual responsibility. What I encode will reflect to some degree on the biological, psychological, and social aspects of my life, and what is encoded will shrink or expand or suffer other transformation in the light of my changing conception of the world I inhabit. Verbal interaction will be the means by which what I encode will be shaped and stored, and my choice will come to influence what counts as experience in the social group to which I belong. Volosinov uses the term *behavioral ideology* to distinguish this level of activity from the *established ideology* represented by institutions—the press, literature, science, etc.—which is a more stable system, yet one that relies for its vitality upon the support of behavioral ideologies.

Volosinov introduces this notion of individual initiative early in the first chapter of his book, *Marxism and the Philosophy of Language* (1973):

> Although the reality of a word, as is true of any sign, resides between individuals, a word, at the same time, is produced by the individual organism's own means without recourse to any equipment or any other kind of extracorporeal material. This has determined the role of word as *the semiotic material of inner life—of consciousness* (inner speech). (p. 14)

Finally, Volosinov tackles what he regards as "one of the most important problems in the science of meanings, the problem of the *interrelationship between meaning and evaluation*." He stresses that the overriding purpose in speaking is an *evaluative* purpose: "All referential contents produced in living speech are said or written with a specific *evaluative* accent. There is no such thing as word without evaluative accent." (p. 103).

Having embarked on an attempt to specify the purposes of literature, I must now go on to raise a question that Volosinov does not at this point consider: What are the consequences of an evaluative utterance upon the choice of subsequent action on the part of the speaker? If for example an experimental inquiry fails to yield any evidence upon the hypothesis that underlay it, what effect might that be expected to have on the inquirer? Will he/she merely reframe the hypothesis in alternative terms and try again? Or might the failure matter so much that life no longer seems worth living? (And of course there have been cases of such disillusionment.) I believe we would have to conclude that what is evaluated in any, broadly speaking scientific activity is likely to be within limits prescribed by professional practice and epistemological levels, or the current state of knowledge in a field.

Consider in contrast the evaluative scope of such a document as the suicide note discovered and reported by Aldous Huxley in *Texts and Pretexts* (1932): "No wish to die. One of the best sports, the boys will tell you. This b, at Palmers Green has sneaked my wife, one of the best in the world; my wife, the first love in the world" (p. 139).

Not that I wish to call that heartfelt cry *literature,* but I would claim that it represents a type of discourse that is in every way responsive to human evaluative needs—and a type of discourse that is capable of the highly sophisticated and influential expression we cannot fail to recognize as literature.

Such discourse, across such a range, must be seen to occupy a key place in the functions of language, and to be of vital importance not simply to addicts, scholars, writers, and critics, but to every man, woman, and child alive in a literate society.

As a postscript to this section of my account, and a truce in the handling of abstractions, let me offer a brief autobiographical fragment, something I produced—by chance—a few days ago. The final product—thirteen lines of verse—is clearly a personal evaluation on my part. Arriving at it was a complex process—the one-line opening cadence came quickly to the pen, but what followed was more of a check than a spur. In transition from inner speech to verbal speech two words surfaced that proved to be unacceptable—for an interesting reason. Here is the whole story:

It was early evening on a September day: I had fallen asleep on the sofa and when I woke I had, momentarily, some glimpse from a fading dream—or perhaps some image germane to the half-waking state. I wrote a line which seemed a way of approaching what I wanted to say—*Opening my eyes on the half-light of an autumn evening*—and I needed to find a way of suggesting that the world I awoke to seemed one which I could appropriately share with the recent dead—the family and companions whom I had outlived. The logic—if logic could be found—lay in the idea that the difference between us was one of timescale rather than total severance—and the evidence for that lay in the extent to which aspects of what had survived them as legacy made up a great part of my environment.

I struggled with the second line that should approach that idea: one attempt began *Here were . . .*—but as I worked on that construction (which above all involved *listening to it*—"word speaking to word") I became aware that it already carried *somebody else's meaning*; that is to say, it was another of those powerful remembered cadences that I have discussed on previous occasions. I tried to fill out that recalled fragment: I surmised that what followed the words *Here were* in the original were words that described features of some landscape long familiar to the writer—but that the recollection would be short-lived, some other image supervening. By now I had Dylan Thomas clearly in mind—thence to *Poem in October*—and recall of that line that made the break: *But the weather turned around.* So I went to the source and found what I wanted:

> A springful of larks in a rolling
> Cloud and the roadside bushes brimming with whistling
> Blackbirds and the sun of October
> Summery
> On the hill's shoulder,
> Here were fond climates and sweet singers suddenly
> Come in the morning where I wandered and listened
> To the rain wringing
> Wind blow cold
> In the wood faraway under me.

—and then—at the end of the following stanza—

> There could I marvel
> My birthday
> Away but the weather turned around.

Had the recollected fragment been such words as *A springful of larks* I should probably have known the source at once. What is interesting is that so semantically neutral a phrase—so simply structural a signal—as *here were* should have that evocative power. I wondered whether it was the tautness of the whole construction— *Here were such and such suddenly come*—that made it memorable. But as I realized this I remembered some of the other fragments that had shown the same characteristics—the same memorableness: *but not this* from Auden's poem *Taller today we remember similar evenings*; from Wallace Stevens' poem *The Idea of Order at Key West*, the skeletal fragment *and I knew that we should . . . ? . . . often. for . . . ? . . .* ; and a similar algebraic formula from Auden's *Age of Anxiety, Whether by A or by B, in X or in Y (English Education, 19(2),* 1987, pp.83–4). What I must conclude is that the structural framework— the grammatical forms that enter such expressions are a more powerful part of the total literary experience than we usually reckon.

This, no doubt, is something I should do well to bear in mind in returning to the production of the second and subsequent lines of my poem on waking. However, as I did so, it seemed evident that my original opening—*here were*—beckoned too strongly in the direction of Dylan Thomas's poem to suit my purposes.

Here is the outcome:

> Opening my eyes on the half-light of an autumn evening
> I was newly aware that the world I inhabit
> Is a world I can share with the recent dead—
> The family and friends whom I dared to outlive.
>
> I knew that their presence survives, alive in the words
> And the tones of their voices; in their sudden appearances—

Claiming a thought, a step in the argument,
A move in the game . . . And it seemed

That what holds us apart is no more than a time-warp,
A trick of the clock that time will correct:
Then those who outlive me—family and friends—
Will join in the dialogue
And mine will be one of the voices they hear.

A first draft and as such, still open to the kinds of complication that refinement of the forms—lexical and syntactic—might produce: though, to tell the truth, my mode of writing does rely more on "shaping at the point of utterance" than it does on refinement by revision.

It is the nature of inner speech as bearer of experience that concerns me in offering this example: the persistence of that remembered phrase from Dylan Thomas despite its seeming paucity of meaning, and the way fresh experience—the dream-like recognition of a conviviality with the recent dead—is realized in terms of the resources inner speech provides.

Chapter Two

A Note on Make-Believe and Mummery

I believe it is part of normal development that children enact narrative meanings before they are able to narrate. It probably counts as a stage in the process of shedding egocentrism—what in Piagetian terms would be an aspect of the growth of intelligence.

Perhaps it can be most clearly illustrated at a late stage in the transition. Polly, the daughter of an Australian colleague working on writing research at the London Institute of Education, was in bed, alone in her room, at the age of three and a half, and she was tape recorded talking to herself—talking, it seems, to keep her spirits up. The fact that her family had recently received news of her grandfather's death in Australia is reflected in her talk:

> Once upon a time there was a story about Goldilocks. She . . .
> She— No—Once there was a girl called . . . Dorothy. She lived in
> London and . . . and she didn't know what to do 'cos she didn't have
> any brothers, dogs, or mothers or fathers or boys. Her grandfather
> was dead. Her mother . . . had died . . . in the same place . . . so
> nobody in the whole world wasn't dead—dead—they were all dead
> . . . So . . . once a little girl came—she wasn't dead. All the girls
> weren't dead and they played with Dorothy and they said 'I will stay
> with you 'cos you're so lonely. And we will live with our (?). We will
> cheer you up and stay with you for ever.' "Thank you," Dorothy
> said—'Thank you' said Dorothy . . . *So* Dorothy went (?) . . . left and
> then (*in a stage whisper*) a ghost came . . . (?) away in another
> country. (*An indecipherable growled sentence then a long silence*)

13

Mm . . .*so*—a very old man who went—he wasn't dead—he didn't know—so he went to Dorothy and he said—and she said, 'My mother has died, my dad, my dad has died. Could you look after me for ever?' 'Yes, my dear . . . Yes, yes my . . .'

Polly lives in her story and moves with it. At no point, I think, does she detach herself enough to fulfill the narrator's role—rather, she is an actor in the scene. The voice tones heard on the recording support this interpretation: there is a good deal of speaking in character, especially—but not only—the character of a scared little girl who is sorry for herself!

There is of course evidence of the ability of three-year-olds to tell a story—to move outside the action and *narrate*. But here it is an enacted narrative form that Polly employs.

Laurie, at two years one month, represents a much earlier stage of enactment. Her four-word script (*Come; Bonk; More; Gone*) enacts no story until you realize that she is watching from the window as two dustmen come through the gate, one after the other, and deposit two dustbins with a clang:

> *Come* she says as they enter;
> *Bonk* for the first dustbin;
> *More* for the second;
> *Gone.*

This is certainly not narrative speech, and perhaps it will be argued that there is no enactment, but I believe that would be to draw too fine a line between enacting a response and enacting an original thought.

Enactment, as Bruner (1975) has demonstrated, plays a key role at a pre-language stage of development. Routines, or formats, usually originated by the mother, are adopted—and modified—by the child and become his/her first intentional mode of communicating meaning. "Pat-a-cake pat-a-cake" is a simple early example. The routines will tend to emphasize closure, a point of arrival, as a means of singling out a segment of behavior: thus, "Where's Laurie?" followed by *"There she is!"*—covering and uncovering her face. In early stages the adult supplies the speech, but later it is taken over by the child. Bruner observes the giving and receiving game (often originating when a child drops a toy and an adult picks it up and returns it) and traces the stages by which the child gradually, over a period of months, takes over the appropriate spoken accompaniment—for example, "There you are!" when giving and "Thank you!" on receiving. As enacted meanings over a range of occasions are paired, in the child's mind, with the spoken utterances he/she hears (or speaks), it seems reasonable to speculate that this constitutes an essential key to using and understanding language.

A particular feature of pre-language enactment, and one shared with the higher apes—the "subhuman primates"—is what the anthropologists have called "the play face" (Bruner, Jolly, & Sylva 1976). This is a phenomenon that has been observed by many students of chimpanzees and baboons. Bruner reports:

> It turns out that play is universally accompanied in subhuman primates by a recognizable form of meta-signaling, a "play face." . . . It is a powerful signal—redundant in its features, which include a particular kind of open-mouthed gesture, a slack but exaggerated gait, and a marked "galumphing" in movement. (p. 14)

Laurie, my first grandchild, comes back into the story as my example of this phenomenon—the only one I have any experience of. I reported the occurrence at the time as follows (Britton, 1983):

> I had picked up enough about anthropologists' use of the term to be interested in the phenomenon when it appeared, though it was my daughter (who knew nothing at all of the matter) who first noticed it. "Have you seen Laurie duck?" she asked, "to be comic, to be un-serious?" Laurie was one year fifteen weeks old at the time, and we duly witnessed the performance. The "duck" was a kind of crouch, as though an attempt to get nearer the ground: her shoulders raised, her head at an angle. Her face wore a peculiar expression, slightly apprehensive, as though to say, "You *do* know I'm only playing"; and her gait was what my daughter described as a Groucho walk. In this stance on this occasion she proceeded to do what she dearly loved to do, but knew it was forbidden—she went to the nearest bookcase and began pulling books out on to the floor! A little later—another forbidden delight, similarly "protected"— she went over to fiddle with the knobs on the television set. (p. 3)

Bruner (1975, p. 355) includes in his volume a reference to the similarity of the "play face" in primates to "rough-and-tumble" play among nursery school children, but Laurie's case seems to represent a clear example of a young child enacting a role dictated to her, not by observing the habits of others but by some inner, inherited necessity. It must surely be accounted an early example of conveying a meaning by enactment—and one that stands at the furthest remove from deliberate, socially motivated behavior.

The early work of A. R. Luria (1956, 1971) drew attention to the stage at which, usually around the age of three years, children begin to be able to understand and use words *non-synpraxically*—that is to say, outside the immediate context. Words begin to stand in place of things, to the vast enrichment of what language can do—bringing the remembered past to bear upon the concerns of the moment. Clearly this marks the earliest beginnings of the ability to participate in an event while it is taking place and then to *represent* it, communicating it by enactment. Successive steps that render the representation less subjectively—to record or report it rather than to rehearse it—must mark the progress to straightforward narration. A study of the records of my two granddaughters up to the age of three or four makes it quite clear that their talk at that stage is either synpraxic—here-and-now talk, referring only to what is present in the immediate environment—or it originates in make-believe play activity. In that context, it builds up in the course of time in its own set of familiar terms. The talk recorded earlier, showing Laurie setting out a make-believe situation (p. 6) employs rich resources of affective terms: "Now its time for little darlings to go to sleep." But from time to time in such exchanges the flow of dialogue is interrupted by what are essentially stage directions. These are clearly products of the constructive imagination, but they take on more and more of the factual informative role. Here is an example of Laurie at four years three months:

L: Now. I'm the mummy. I'm the school-teacher mummy. First you've got to be a little girl or a little boy. Sit down in the classroom. Now, what have you been doing at school today? Have you any . . . Pretend you're 15 . . . um . . . We're going in the hall today.

Me: Doing some gymnastics?

L: No—Yes we will, but—try and not to hit your foot and hurt your toe. . . cos. . . on the bars. . . cos . . . (pause) Now— pretend you've got to be somebody else now. Don't go on the bars. Pretend you will when I say don't.

Me: Oh I've hurt my toe on the bars! What shall I do?

L: *(angrily)* You shouldn't have trod on the bar. Well, you'll have to go to hostipal (sic) cos you've been silly and gone on the bars.

In course of time, the references to the real world will tend to be in factual tones, reporting circumstances of the action, not as rehearsal but as narrative, a form which tends to neutralize the distinction between a factual account of events and fictional narrative. But I would suspect that in the speech of men and women of all ages, reenactment is likely to be an element in a great many accounts of real or supposed encounters. The fact that such variations are likely to persist as random recurrent features would accord with the view that whatever we relate of experience must inevitably carry our evaluative coloring. We have only to hear someone enraged by an insult giving his/her account of the event to feel the element of enactment.

I began with Polly at three and a half years of age and then worked backwards to the origins of narrative enactment in early infancy. Where is this development headed? If narrative conveyed by enactment reflects the performer's difficulty in detaching the teller from the tale, does that suggest that the target performance is impersonal or dispassionate narration?

I think it is much more complicated than that. The key, I believe, lies in the fact that narration demands the use of the language of propositions—sentences that make statements—whereas enactment is possible without that. Laurie's scene from the window, for example, as explicitly narrated rather than implied by enactment, would require some such propositions as:

> This man came in.
> He banged down a dustbin.
> Another man came.
> They both went away.

Mastery of propositional language is a major advance for the language learner. If we are to believe Michel Foucault (1973), "The threshold of language lies at the point where the verb first appears" (p. 93). Citing the verb *to be* as representative, he goes on to define its function as

> that which, by enabling language to affirm what it says, renders it susceptible of truth or error. In this respect it is different from all the signs that may or may not be consistent with, faithful to, or well adapted to, what they designate, but that are never true or false. Language is, wholly and entirely, *discourse*; and it is so by virtue of this singular power of a word to leap across the system of signs towards the being of what is signified. (p. 94)

Propositional language affirms what it states and thus, as things work out, offers to the listener two choices: It may be taken as information about the world we operate in, and as such accepted as true, questioned, or dismissed as false; or it may be taken as a hypothetical statement or as fantasy—a statement to be entertained, considered, enjoyed, but not believed. But do we always know which response is appropriate, and when does a child learn to distinguish?

I am reminded that from the age of two and a half years, when Laurie's concerns actively embraced both make-believe and the social realities of family life, she showed considerable interest in the relation of the true to the "pretend." She was puzzled, for example, as to whether the sound of her voice on the tape recorder was "a pretend Laurie" or a real one, and in her make-believe games, say in feeding her toy creatures, she took care, for a time, to attach the prefix *pretend* to imagined items such as scrambled eggs, etc.. Further, my earlier records of Clare at the age of two and three quarters included her agonized comment about her toy farm:"Daddy, *why* am I so *real* so I can't live in my little farm?"

In fact, as we have seen (p. 6), a number of observers have remarked on the way children develop at an early age a receptivity that differentiates fantasy from reality and responds to each appropriately. Propositional language, once acquired, may serve then to strengthen their ability to distinguish *what is* from *what seems*. We have to recognize, I am sure, that make-believe play, in addition to creating an imagined context for a great deal of enjoyable activity, does at the same time constitute the generation of hypotheses about the nature of reality and an element of rehearsal of the appropriate responses to that reality.

So with the help of propositional language, storytelling develops and no longer relies exclusively upon enactment, though this may continue to act as a lively means of securing and holding an audience. Enactment itself takes a more and more prominent role in face-to-face encounters—selectively in the sense that some of us employ it much more than others do. There are conversationalists who *become*—by tones of voice, gestures, body language—one after the other the people whose actions or views they retail. Thus the function of enactment in children's early make-believe play leads directly both to social role-taking and to dramatic improvisation— and with some speakers, the one may move easily into the other.

Dramatic improvisation is normally a collective activity but, where circumstances prevent that, it may take the form of a solitary performance (as, for example, in the *spiel* I refer to on page 5). There seems to be a certain continuity in modes of performing; what tends to change from one situation to another, and from one age-level to another, is awareness of audience and its effect on the performers. In the primary school, for example, improvisation may seem a game well worth playing, while in the secondary school the stimulus of the audience may be a necessary component.

An aspect of growth in adolescence is the search for a life pattern—for concerns and activities that both individuate and communalize the youngster. With reference to the arts, this is likely to involve a growing involvement in a particular form of artistic activity, whether it be drawing or painting, music, dance, poetry, or maybe the novel—and certainly this happens with regard to dramatic activity, perhaps particularly so on account of the attraction or rejection by the individual of its gregarious and convivial nature.

It is difficult to understand why dramatic activity should feature so strongly in some secondary schools in England and Wales and yet find little support in the United States; and this in spite of educational recognition of the social importance of such activity in democratic society (Moffett, 1968; Rouse, 1978). Perhaps the historical continuity from early religious drama through Shakespearean times to the present day theater has preserved a readiness for personally accessible forms of dramatic activity. And perhaps the cinema—wherever it flourishes—acts in a contrary direction, fostering a sense that dramatic activity is a highly professional and costly activity.

Community theater—a neighborhood activity in which a considerable number of nonprofessional actors may take part—is still alive in Britain, a tradition tenuously linked to the performances of medieval times. Not more than a year or two ago, for example, the Dorchester Community Theater gave local performances celebrating events in West Country history and were encouraged by members of the National Theater to bring the play to London, which they did with considerable success. Moreover, in very widespread and diverse ways, amateur play production, supported by friends and relations and celebrated in the columns of local newspapers, continues.

The social role of the theater and the performing arts in general has become the subject of sociological and critical speculation. The writer and critic J. I. M. Stewart (1949) commented on the nature of theater as a collective experience; a spell, a kind of social hypnotism while the performance lasts—call it corporate apperception, perhaps. He explains the nature of the spell with reference to the climax of Shakespeare's *Anthony and Cleopatra*. It is a very moving scene he suggests,

> but assuredly no man on leaving the theater ever thrust his wet handkerchief angrily away and ground his teeth at being cozened by a counterfeit of human passion. On the contrary, we are convinced of a profound significance in what we have witnessed. And we may assert—contemplating still the close of the play—that our impression of truth in the fable results not from an illusion the poetry creates but from an actual correlation between high dramatic poetry and insight into substantial human nature. For true poetry is emotion differentiating, is passion clarifying itself, in the contemplation of these activities. (p. 77)

Poetic drama displays a protagonist's potential to break free from habitual thought and patterns of behavior and in so doing to create in the collective audience a disposition to accept such, if only for the time being, as true to human nature. The poetic text results, as

Stewart claims, from an existing relationship between what the drama indicates and what living experience affirms.

Theatrical performance certainly offers a kind of experience that individuals on their own do not easily acquire; and perhaps that is of particular relevance in a community where joint social undertakings are less likely to flourish. With such speculations in mind, I believe the infant's early experiments in enacting aspects of their experience may be seen to bear lifetime benefits.

Chapter Three

Heads or Tales

Volosinov asserted that speech that refers to experience almost universally has an evaluative component. The piece I wrote in the postscript to Chapter one was certainly a reflective piece, but it has a broadly narrative structure—it told of what I did on a September evening and of something that happened to me. I say "reflective," but in particular it was *evaluative*. My concern on this occasion was a pretty solemn one, offering an evaluation not only of life itself but also of death. We shall more often find ourselves assessing the value to us of a more mundane or even trivial aspect of experience—the flavor of a dish, the force of a word, the duration of a delay.

I have often thought it surprising how frequently a novelist opens his or her story by reporting characters exchanging views on some event or piece of behavior. I suppose it provides a demonstration of the emotional coloring of relationships that are to figure in the story, at the same time sketching in relevant events and perhaps giving an indication of the arena within which they will principally take place. Examples come readily to hand; here is the opening of Virginia Woolf's *To the Lighthouse*

> "Yes, of course, if it's fine tomorrow," said Mrs. Ramsay. "But you'll have to be up with the lark," she added.
>
> To her son these words conveyed an extraordinary joy, as if it were settled the expedition were bound to take place, and the wonder to which he had looked forward, for years and years it seemed, was, after a night's darkness and a day's sail, within touch.
>
> (p. 3)

The arena indicated is one of domestic events, fraught by the contrasting relations within the family—Mrs. Ramsay's "yes of course" is soon met head on by her husband's " 'But,' said his father, stopping in front of the drawing-room window, 'it won't be fine.' " And there is a sense in which the whole episode—the journey to the lighthouse—provides a framework that encompasses Mrs. Ramsay's death and the effect that has upon the family.

In the opening of Tolstoy's *War and Peace*, we forgo family forecasts of the weather and find instead the political futilities of aristocratic Russian Society—still, however, turning on personal relationships, but in response to the destinies of nations:

> Eh bien, mon prince, so Genoa and Lucca are now no more than private estates of the Bonaparte family. No—I warn you—if you are not telling me that this means war, if you again allow yourself to condone all the infamies and atrocities perpetuated by that Antichrist (upon my word I believe he is Antichrist) I don't know you in future. You will no longer be a friend of mine. (p. 3)

I believe it is essential to bear in mind that the evaluative function provides what amounts to a verdict on whether or not life is worth living for us. What is judged on any single occasion may be comparatively trivial, but in sum total such judgments may constitute a matter of life or death, and we underestimate their importance—to ourselves or to other people—if we fail to acknowledge this fact.

Stories come in may guises and serve a variety of purposes; some narratives barely deserve to be called stories at all, since values and evaluating have no shaping effect upon the form of their telling. Time-sequenced factual description of a process would be in this category—say an outline account of how a petrol engine works.

We might make a rough distinction between true stories and fictional ones, but we should recognize that what these categories represent would be stages on a continuum rather than self-contained distinct groups—the most factual account must rely to some extent upon guesswork and supposition.

In calling this chapter *Heads or Tales*—by which *heads* indicates either headings or headlines—the kind of informative statement likely to occur is contrasted with a narrative—a story. It seems worth inquiring how far these modes of communicating the reasons for our actions differ and how far they overlap.

What is involved appears most clearly in such contexts as medical or psychiatric records or ethnographic studies. Take, for example, a work by Oliver Sacks, the purpose of which is to present cases of mental sickness—not in the usual mode of psychiatric records, but in such a way as to "restore the human subject at the center." (1987) "We must deepen a case-history to a narrative or tale," he writes in his introduction to *The Man Who Mistook His Wife for a Hat* (p. viii). I was very much struck when I read the book, a few years ago, by its distinctive narrative style. While in fact a collection of actual case studies, its narrative mode is very unlike the diagnostic, technically worded—confidentiality minded—case-studies generally to be found in psychoanalytic texts. In fact, in reading it I was responding as though it were fiction and from time to time I suffered a shock in discovering that the authorities occasionally referred to were real people whose names I knew: the Soviet psychologist A. R. Luria, for example, whose work I have frequently quoted. Moreover, these full narrative accounts, unlike most psychiatric studies, seem to pay no heed to the recognizability of the men and women whose "cases" were described. What stood out above all, however, was the power of the narratives to engage my imagination, and enlist my sympathies and understanding as no analytic report could have done.

In a recent interview, Sacks was asked what features of imaginative literature he considered of value in medical description. "It's the very detailed representation of experience in fiction, its truth to life," he claimed."I think one cannot describe physiological processes without this kind of phenomenological detail. Without it we actually cannot understand what it is to be alive." (Ryle, 1990).

These same contrasting modes of portrayal are illustrated in another account of a psychoanalytic encounter, the story of a young doctor's training and early experience. In *The Call of Stories* (1989), Robert Coles seems to have the perspective of an English professor, but, as the dust cover tells us, he is Professor of Psychiatry and Medical Humanities at Harvard. The chapter that caught my attention was the first, which Coles calls "Stories and Theories." It is the account of how, as a trainee psychoanalyst working in a hospital, he was supervised by two other senior doctors; the first of whom urged him to formulate the patient's problems, study the 'psychodynamics' of the case, read up on the appropriate psychiatric literature; the second reminded him that "The people who come to see us bring us their stories. They hope they tell them well enough so that we understand the truth of their lives. We have to remember that what we hear is *their* story." And it was this second advisor who later suggested that the young doctor should abandon the psychiatric interview in favor of something nearer to a conversation—a conversation with the emphasis on listening to what the patient has to say.

By the end of this chapter Cole's opinion is quite clear: telling the stories of our lives is always capable of conveying reality in a way that no theoretical formulation could match. He points out to us, in passing, that the word *theory* itself springs from a Greek root *theamai*, meaning "I behold"—indicating that a theory, in this original sense, should be a way of interpreting what has been *observed*. In contrast, it seems to me the presentation of a case description in theoretical terms tends very often to suggest a "closing down"—a claim, perhaps, for the last word. A narrative presentation, on the other hand, is more likely to suggest an "opening up"—an invitation to others to consider motives and effects, and indeed participate by making their own comments.

The commercial use of narrative as argument—that is to say, as means of persuasion—must be as old as advertising (and as up-to-date as this afternoon's television programs, worldwide). Its history, of course, goes back far beyond such uses; it seems unlikely that there are holy books in any religion that have not tempted readers into piety of one brand or another by means of stories illustrating the good life that follows from "proper" conduct or the pitfalls that attend its denial.

That stories may move us by working upon our feelings, as well as convincing by evidence, was an issue raised in the great anti-slavery lobby in England in the early nineteenth century. In 1823, Sir Thomas Buxton, philanthropist and Member of Parliament, wrote to a friend:

> "You are of the opinion that the public is so sagacious a creature as to require only bare facts, that he wants no more ornament or entertainment than a mathematician. Now believe me, the public neither can nor will receive into his obtuse understanding anything which is not conveyed through the medium of his imagination or his feelings; and if you want to move him, you must address yourself to those only openings through which he is assailable." (Buxton, 1848)

On the other hand, we are told that William Wordsworth—probably in that same year—when a Sheffield lady invited him to contribute to an anthology of anti-slavery pieces that she was compiling, replied: "Poetry if good for anything must appeal forcibly to the imagination and the feelings; but what, at this period, we want above everything is patient examination and sober judgment" (N. B. Lewis, 1934, p. 14).

Whether Wordsworth's refusal denotes a less cynical view of his fellow men than Thomas Buxton's, there can be no question that the influence they accord to an appeal to reasonable argument sketches in familiar battle lines of long-standing conflict—where the protagonists are stories on the one hand and theories on the other.

How far, then, can we carry the substitution of the one for the other? Can the record of events carry its own unambiguous interpretation as to what may be the outcome?

When at the London Institute of Education, the team carrying out the Schools Council Research on the development of writing abilities was working to devise categories in which to classify the functions of school writing and the audiences to whom it was addressed. We aimed at getting the best of both worlds by formulating what we called *an anecdotal taxonomy*—the term suggested, I believe, by Peter Wexler from the University of Essex. The idea intrigued us, set us a puzzle worth pondering, but in the end eluded us. I wonder today what we could have made of it. I suppose at least it indicated the attempt to establish categories of purpose in writing and categories of intended audiences based on observed examples seen in practice. In any event, it appeared to constitute a self-denying ordinance: Whereas any verbally formulated statement has to be interpreted, category definition by narrative would surely work more by implication than by explicit statement. The category boundaries, that is to say, might remain dependent upon some consanguinity between the code setter and code user. We set out to produce categories that could prove useful to all teachers without elaborate training, but it is not difficult to see now on looking back that this entails an assessment of the user's ability to interpret category definitions that involve varying degrees of practical experience, interpretative ability, and reasoning powers. It was at least valuable to have had before us the possible use of a taxonomy that was anecdotal.

Our category definitions—often enough descriptions rather than definitions—did at times appeal to the imagination and practical common sense of readers, using conversational language and making reference to story-like situations. For example, use of the expressive category in writing included the following:

(a) Writing addressed to a limited public audience assumed to share much of the writer's context and many of his values and opinions and interests (e.g., "interest" articles in specialist journals, gossip columns).

(b) Writing, intended to be read by a public audience, in which the writer chooses to approach his reader as though he were a personal friend, hence revealing much about himself by implication in the course of dealing with his topic.

Clearly, operational definitions of this kind profit from a specificity, a degree of control over interpretation that the force of a story may lack. It is certainly true, however, that knowledge and understanding may be greatly enhanced when, taking a cue from the manner in which we gain wisdom from the events that make up our lives, we communicate by offering our accounts of events as data for others to interpret.

It would be a mistake to see these two modes of informing as competing; rather, they fulfill different requirements. Vygotsky (1978, p. 51) has explained how early memory in childhood may take the form of a chronicle of events, but it must very soon become "logicalized" if it is to carry the density of information we accumulate and need to call upon as adolescents and adults: memory must in fact become "the storehouse of *what must have been*" rather than the catalogue of *what was*. And Michael Polanyi's conception of "personal knowledge" (1958) embraces both tacit knowledge (that which can be put into words); and traces modes of conversion by which explicit knowledge may gain some ground by converting tacit knowledge to explicit.

Unquestionably, to speak in terms that cite experience is to stay close to the daily habits of mind of most people. And even the most learned of discourse may well value the flash of enlightenment that can result when an author both *shows* what he means as well as defines it.

In *Actual Minds, Possible Words* (1986) Bruner makes it clear that in his dealings with story, it is "narrative as an art form" that he intends (p. 15). There are in the chapters that follow many highly perceptive observations on the qualities evinced by literary narrative, but at no point does the author attempt to define what makes a narrative an art form or what would define narrative utterances that are not works of art. This tends, I believe, to encourage a view that narrative and literature may be terms for the same thing.

An attempt to distinguish the one from the other might begin, somewhat paradoxically, with the study of "oral versions of personal experience"—a narrative analysis carried out by William Labov and Joshua Waletzky (1967). Their premise was this: "In our opinion, it will not be possible to make very much progress in the analysis and understanding of . . . complex narratives until the simplest and most fundamental structures are analyzed in direct connection with their originating functions" (p. 12). They thus set out to collect the stories told by unsophisticated speakers, encountered on the streets of New York City, in response to such questions as: "Were you ever in a situation where you thought you were in serious danger of getting killed?" (p. 14) or "What was the most important fight you remember?" (p. 17) etc. The researchers define narrative by its function, as "one verbal technique for recapitulating experience" (p. 20): "a technique of constructing narrative units which match the temporal sequence of that experience" (p. 13). The narrators (numbering about six hundred in all) "include speakers from Negro and White communities, rural and urban areas, and they range in age from 10 to 72 years old" (p. 13). There were no highly educated speakers among them.

It seems reasonable to suppose that the casual nature of the speech situation would make it very unlikely that respondents would have any practical or utilitarian purpose in mind as they spoke; the overt function was that of recalling experience in response to the questioner's interest.

Analysis of the recorded stories was conducted clause by clause. First, any clause that was in temporal sequence (matching the sequence of events reported) was deemed to be a *narrative clause*. Inspection of the remaining clauses, those that were not in temporal sequence, and hence were free to occur over a range of the narrative, led to the conclusion that their function was *evaluative*. Moreover, when stories were found that had no evaluative clauses—and nothing by way of evaluation within the narrative clauses—they were found to be *"empty or pointless narratives."*

This detailed analysis of the collected narratives led the authors to draw up rules that govern typical spoken narratives of personal experience. They found the overall structure of these to feature:

1. Orientation: optional free clauses (i.e., not part of the narrative sequence) that introduce a listener to such aspects as persons, place, time, and behavioral situation. ("When I was in fourth grade—no—it was third grade—there was this boy . . .")

2. Complication: comprising the main body of narrative clauses, presenting the events terminating in some "result" or effect. ("I say, 'Calvin, I'm bust your head for dat.' Calvin stuck his head out. I th'ew the rock, and the rock went up, I mean went up, came down, and say (slap), and smacked him in the head, and his head busted.")

3. Evaluation: "that part of the narrative which reveals the attitude of the narrator towards the narrative by emphasizing the relative importance of some narrative units as compared to others" (p. 37). A narrative that does not include evaluation is not a complete narrative; it remains difficult to interpret and lacks significance. Many of the narratives stress the unexpected or unusual nature of an experience—and it is this aspect that may be highlighted in the evaluation. ("And naturally, the first thing was—run to the doctor. And the doctor just says, 'Just about this much more,' he says 'and you'd a been dead.' ")

4. Resolution: when narrative clauses follow an evaluation, reporting an event, or events, that corroborate the anticipated outcome, this is an example of a resolution (e.g., a narrative about the search of a missing woman ends with the statement "But—however—that settled it for the day").

5. Coda: Many narratives have this additional feature, a device for bringing the verbal statement up to the present time—by one of a variety of means not intrinsically associated with the events narrated.

The role allotted to evaluation by Labov and Walezky in the structure of spoken accounts of personal experience provides an important basis for considering the nature of "gossip," or casual chat, in a more general person-to-person conversation.

An important study that seeks to relate such conversation—familiar talk about people and events—to works of literature is that by D. W. Harding: first in a *Scrutiny* article (1937), "The Role of the Onlooker," and later (1962) in *The British Journal of Aesthetics*, "Psychological Processes in the Reading of Fiction." His concept of "the role of spectator" as the stance from which both gossip and the literary story are created is one that we took up and developed as part of our writing model in the London Institute of Education Schools Council research project. To make short work of a long story, *language in the role of participant* designates any use of language to get things done, to pursue the world's affairs, while *language in the role of spectator* covers verbal artifacts, the use of language to *make something*, rather than to *get something done*. However, if the whole span is seen as a continuum along which a particular utterance may be plotted, we seem to require three forms of language to cover the continuum: on one hand, transactional language (at the limit of the participant role), merging into *expressive*–the language of ordinary, informal face-to-face talk (see also p. 25 above)—and that in turn merging into poetic language, the language of literature, of verbal artifacts. It seems worth noting that expressive, informal face-to-face speech may hover uncertainly between participant and spectator roles—gaining from aspects of both.

The diagram shows both language functions, and then language forms:

Language in the role of   Language in the role of

Participant – Spectator

Transactional – – – – – – **Expressive** – – – – – – – – – – – **Poetic**

Applied to narrative, the model will distinguish function and form thus:

Factual process narrative – – – – – – – – – Gossip – – – –The verbal arts
Circumstantial evidence in court   about events
[Transactional – – – – – – – – – – – – – – Expressive – – – – – – – Poetic]

We have claimed that activity in the spectator role represents above all a mode of handling the data of experience—an activity of mind that parallels the physical processes of metabolism. If the world we operate in is shaped by the way we represent it to ourselves, then it must follow that the means we employ to maintain the unity, coherence, and harmony of that representation—its truth to experience as we have felt it—must be of lasting concern to each of us.

A recent review of this work by Russel Durst and George Newell (1989) comments on this aspect of the research: "Perhaps one of the most controversial suggestions Britton has made concerning poetic uses of language is that the work of the poet and the storytelling of the child are unified by a common purpose: the symbolic representation of experience through language." (p. 390). And they go on to note that the poetic function is not here defined in terms of text elements but rather in the uses to which it is put: in writing or reading, speaking or listening—both formally in works of literature and informally in conversational exchange. "While Bloom and Hirsch seem to be arguing for the transmission of a static culture," they conclude, "the tradition that Britton speaks for is one in which culture can be reinterpreted, reunderstood, and made anew" (p 391).

I think the essential feature of the reinterpretation the individual can achieve lies in recognizing that it is our own estimate of life's chances—the opportunities and expectations, the costs, the penalties and the misapprehensions—that will continue to guide us.

Spectator role activities, that particular type of reflection-by-reenactment, must constitute a continuing sense as to whether life, for us, is worth living. And it is by the stories that people tell of themselves that we may catch the first signs of a distress signal. Let me quote the widely known and well documented case of the fifteen-year-old American schoolboy, whose story begins by claiming, as we might also claim that "he always wanted to explain things":

> He always wanted to explain things.
> But no one cared.
> So he drew.
> Sometimes he would draw
> And it wasn't anything.

He wanted to carve it in stone
or write it in the sky,
and it would be only him and the sky and
the things inside him that needed saying.
It was after that he drew the picture.
It was a beautiful picture.
He kept it under his pillow
and would let no one see it.
He would look at it every night
and think about it.
When it was dark and his eyes were closed,
he could still see it,
When he started school,
he brought it with him,
not to show anyone,
just to have along like a friend.
It was funny about school
He sat at a square, brown desk,
Like all the other square, brown desks.
He thought it should be red.
And his room was a square, brown room,
like all the other rooms.
It was tight and close and stiff.
He hated to hold the pencil and chalk,
His arms stiff, his feet flat on the floor,
stiff,
the teacher watching and watching.
The teacher came and spoke to him.
She told him to wear a tie
like all the other boys.
He said he didn't like them.
She said it didn't matter!
After that, they drew.
He drew all yellow.
It was the way he felt about morning,
and it was beautiful.
The teacher came and smiled at him.
"What's this?" she said "Why don't you
draw something like Ken's drawing?
Isn't that beautiful?"
After that, his mother bought him a tie,
and he always drew airplanes and rocketships
like everyone else.
And he threw the old picture away.
And when he lay alone looking at the sky,
it was big and blue and all of everything
but he wasn't anymore
He was square inside and brown,

and his hands were stiff.
He was like everyone else.
The things inside that needed saying
didn't need it anymore.
It has stopped pushing,
It was crushed.
Stiff.
Like everything else.

The first lines—each in a self-contained sentence—seem to me to epitomize the boy's story: understanding one's own experience is a process that relies upon sharing problems and trying out solutions—a social undertaking. Taken together, those first two statements set up an opposition.

If, as he sees it, his search for understanding meets no response from those around him, the version of experience he must create for himself will be a private world: what he "creates in the sky" will be "only him . . . and things inside him that need saying." Its reality is in a secret world, one he can still see in the dark, yet allows no one else a glimpse of. And school—a rough-and-tumble world, a world of give and take, of compromise and making do—will find his private reality intractable: to the point where, for him, the private world breaks down—and the urge itself to explain things is silenced. What is amazing—it seems to me—is how much of that confrontation the writer himself perceives, and how well he presents the story of it.

It is a primary function of language in the role of spectator to be constantly concerned with the corpus of an individual's experience: that corpus, as I called it twenty years ago, "that generates the pluses and minuses of his fluctuating verdict on the world, his fluctuating acceptance of the human condition, his fluctuating faith in himself" (Britton, 1971, pp. 218-19).

The retreat into a solitary world, a private world, did in fact amount to a cry of distress for this fifteen-year-old, but it came too late. The psychiatrist who had tried to help him reported that two weeks after writing this piece he committed suicide. She hoped that the piece would be read widely and recognized as an urgent warning to schools, to parents, to society generally. It was first published for that reason by Clare Winnicott, in an article called "Communicating with Children."

But such a story presents, as it were, the concluding chapter: Many people may never have the opportunity, on the one hand, nor suffer despair on the other, that leads to the drawing up of our last word on life. Yet from time to time, and for some people, at frequent intervals, they may have given expression to critical judgments upon aspects of their experience that stand as elements in any final verdict. In fact, it is by such exchanges that we profit from other people's experiences and live, in part, a common life—a life that is subject to common influences and in which we influence each other.

I believe, for example that we could learn a great deal about formal education by hearing the stories that adolescent schoolboys or schoolgirls tell: they are at the receiving end of formal high school education and have had long enough there to adjust to and evaluate its effects.

This fourteen-year-old in a London Comprehensive school—so different in her response to the Illinois schoolboy—has in common the complaint that the community of the classroom is not one in which she is encouraged to discover herself and her potential—is in fact often impatient of the demands of the adolescent. Whether the piece was ever seen by the teacher addressed, I do not know—a student who taught the class for a time was given it to read, and to profit from:

Getting the Message

You gave me a piece of paper, and you said: "Write down the whole story in your own words," and you left me for half an hour and when you came back you were so pleased I handed you two pages of writing. When we sat down you said "I know what you're going through." I wanted to laugh, because you *don't* know, and you're just like every other teacher who's given me a pet talk *(sic)* and like all the others, you probably read my story and thought: "Poor girl" and if you thought it was the truth, you must be thick.

And when you teachers huddle together in the staff room and discuss me in whispered tones, you think I don't know what names you call me. Well, I do, because they've been said to my face before, and it's not as if I bother any more. So I'll sit here and listen patiently, while you reel off the usual, in your sugary, pathetic voice, and when you've finished, I'll say: "Yes ma'am" and "thank you, ma'am." And you'll be so childishly pleased, and you'll think you helped me, but you're wrong, and no one of your sort can help me, because you're in a different generation, and you'll never understand me. So I'll carry on writing pages and pages of semi-truths and I'll laugh at you behind my hair.

I guess the older one gets, the easier it is to believe that there are continuities in living and that in many social communities some of the basic modes of survival—indeed of satisfying day-to-day existence—remain broadly constant within one's lifetime, and despite major changes in some of the circumstances. Such a belief, and attendant attitudes, certainly do not seem credible to the average adolescent or young person: they seem to belie any confidence in a brave new world and are too complacent about the achievements of the old one. For teachers, as the years go by, the gap between themselves and those they teach will widen imperceptibly, and they must adapt to new relationships and new possibilities.

Here is another fourteen-year-old writing to her teacher in a junior high school in Calgary, Alberta. The letter came with a story she was delivering:

> Dear Miss L—,
> I feel I had to write you this little note. Even though it may not show, I am a relatively shy person. I feel by writing a story you give away a little part of yourself. Somehow I feel by keeping my thoughts to myself less will be revealed. Perhaps this is the wrong way to look at things, but this is my opinion and of course, everyone is entitled to one.
> Yours respectfully, M
> P.S. Thank you for reading this. I will be grateful and indebted to you forever.
> P.P.S. I tend to get flowery. Hope you'll understand.

The teacher made a copy of that letter and brought it for me to see because it represented a relationship of trust and a source of confidence to both pupil and teacher. (P.P.S—yes, she did understand!) It must be added that tact and patience are necessary if we are to dissuade students from setting out in their writing to produce what it is they believe the teacher wants and gives credit for, rather than pursuing the insights that the process could yield.

In an ideal world, surely, relationships of many kinds coexist to create a harmony of various interests, a range of ages—across genders and races. Life in reality rarely wears that look, but there are from time to time brave attempts to achieve piecemeal communities aimed in that direction. The life of a school—or indeed other component community—can never amount to the whole of an individual's existence, but it can, in its limited role achieve that harmony of interests when its educational, social, and political ideals are in tune. In a variety of contexts, such ideals were espoused by thinkers such as Martin Buber, Jean Piaget, Carl Rogers—to name those who dominated the scene during my own early teaching.

One more school story, adding its own note—that of the confident young man of eighteen in a London Comprehensive School:

> If you want a word to sum up the adolescent sensations of the experience of his life so far—try confusion, or diversity, or chaos . . .
> There are conflicts and paradoxes too: one moment he (or I) can feel depressed and repressed by anything from this "education" system of petty exams and drudgery, to a more comprehensive sensation

that not only is this education and suburban or provincial life I lead absurdly pointless, but also and more overwhelmingly that life itself is dead and without point—rationalize all you may about god and afterlife. Yet I can flash suddenly from total fatalism and to explosive and intense joy of life, of hopes for changing the world—new societies . . . I often feel I've achieved nothing in life—but the fact that I think as I do, is I suppose some achievement. I have had the usual few affairs and sex but at present I'm still too vain and self-interested to love anyone so that it would do them any good.

I think the prevailing characteristic of all these schoolgirl and schoolboy examples is their basic honesty: We may fail to realize that when they express views and value judgments at variance with our own, but I believe the failure is nonetheless ours. Again, I believe as adults we have to make allowances for the fact that moods will tend to be more absorbing and more variable for the adolescent than they are later in life when they are felt within a context of more sustained and consistent experiences.

What of the stories that teachers tell—about schools, about students, about classroom encounters? I can turn here to what has been, I believe, the most enjoyable teaching I have engaged in in recent years—at the Bread Loaf School of English in Vermont. What I have taught there, several times now, has been a writing-and-reading seminar on the topic "telling the stories of our lives." As a writing workshop, we read to each other drafts of what we have written about our own lives; as a reading seminar, we read and discuss examples of autobiography such as Mike Rose's (1990) *Lives on the Boundary*, autobiographical fiction such as Malcolm Lowry's (1947) *Under the Volcano* and theoretical statements by scholars and writers on the processes and purposes of autobiography—as for example Jerome Bruner's "Life as Narrative" (1988), in which he suggests that the modes of construing in which we relate experiences may come to operate as expectations concerning future experience, with power to influence the course of events themselves.

The mixture—stories and theories, tales and heads—seems to make a powerful amalgam. Many of the pieces chronicle the hopes, the misgivings, the self-doubting, the renewed efforts of young teachers as they fight for a foothold: most show a ready understanding of the "conscientious objectors" to the prevailing system of compulsory education, particularly in situations where minority interests are paramount. Here then are grounds for considerable overlap between the views of the learners and of the teacher-learners. I chose the next piece because a teacher in his first year of teaching, and assigned to a Reservation School, writes of an occasion when he is at a loss, while those he is expected to teach know the score, and may even seem to relish the fact and make the most of it. He appears, in his writing, anxious to share the festive lives of his pupils and unwilling to remain a stranger to the cultural roots that feed them.

> Finally, Stickdance Day arrived and I was glad. I was tired of the students "Stickdance, Stickdance, Stickdance" interrupting the emancipation Proclamation or the imagery of a poem. They refused to tell me about Stickdance, their Ceremony of the Dead. They scorned my questions with blank faces and mumbled denials of knowledge. It made me feel far away.
>
> As we walked to the community hall, the snap of our boots on snow echoed back from the dark. Conversation was sparse, too difficult through scarfs and ruffs. Occasionally, far down the road, a snow-go blared, and we watched its light bounce "back town" for a forgotten dish or kid. When one swept close, ice sparked in its funneled light and we strained to see who hid behind the parka. Clouds blanketed the moon, thank God, or it would have been colder.
>
> When I stepped through the door and into the sweet swelter of smells, my glasses fogged. Carol giggled at my blindness, and as I wiped the frost from my beard, I told her I'd get even in class. She believed me and pushed back into her crowd. "Carol," I wanted to say, "I was only joking." But it was too late; the moment had passed.
>
> I wandered the length of the room, careful not to bump the toddlers as they careened through the crowd, trying to outrun older sisters sent to catch them. The children were dressed in their finest parkas, their black hair tangling in wolverine ruffs. Their fat cheeks glistened with sweat; eyes flashed with excitement. And they were all so quiet—not one cried!

I think the writing moves sensitively through a sequence of changing perspectives, bringing life to each: the first—perhaps resentful—anticipation, a sharp sense of the freezing journey that brought the crowd together, and the festival itself—inviting, but perhaps still capable of "making him feel far away." Through it all is the clear sense of someone *who cares.*

In the next example, another first-year teacher looks back on his beginnings and seems sharply aware of how much he had then to learn—that is to say, by how much he has changed in the course of his initiation. I dare say his life-style as an adolescent did not do a great deal to prepare him for the problems that beset minority youngsters, but he proves a ready and responsible learner.

> So one hot morning in September, with all of three days of classroom observations behind me, I walk into Room 7 at . . . High

School. The class is finishing up a unit on oral reading, which culminates with each student reading a poem to his or her peers and then explaining the meaning of the poem as best he or she could . . .

Most of the readings were lackluster, but a few were animated by a determination and vivacity that impressed me. One young lady read a poem by Alice Walker that is written in black English. She did an admirable job of it; her voice was full of the passion and pain of a world that had been closed to me or inaccessible for a number of reasons, most notably the pervasive, systematic racism of white institutions and white communities. The girl's performance was not greeted with applause by my master teacher, who looked over at me during the reading and rolled his eyes, as if to say, See what I mean? She thinks this is literature.

Since the kids had to read to me, a stranger, I thought it only fair that I read something to them. For the occasion, I had chosen a poem by June Jordan, a visionary and sharp-tongued black poet from NYC . . . The kids seemed to like my reading, which was prefaced by my explanation of who I was, and what I was doing in front of them, and why I wanted to read to them. I strutted my stuff, used a bunch of twenty-dollar words, and fluffed my white feathers.

At the end of the class, as I was gathering my things to return to the university, a student approached me and introduced herself. She was 17, she said, and her name was Rose. "So you're from Berkeley," she said. Yep, I said, proud of myself for meeting this challenge straight on, smiling as if I knew all there was to know about working with kids like Rose.

Before I knew what hit me, Rose began to speak to me in the dialect of black teenagers who grow up in the inner city, in a language that was richly metaphoric, seductive in its rhythms, and syntactically complex. I had a tremendous difficulty deducing her meaning and the confusion on my face must have blazed forth like a neon sign.

When she stopped her "rap", Rose paused a moment, and looked at me squarely. I was speechless. She broke the silence with these words: " 'You don't know everything, do you? You still got a lot to learn. Okay, listen. If you want, I'll help you."

Here the confrontation is presented dramatically, and the writer has cast himself in a derogatory role—one which contrasts with his present views, though no doubt the difference is more rhetorical than realistic—part of the strategy by which the discourse is shaped. In fact, this account in dramatic and narrative form is in marked contrast with the reflective account given by the writer on Stickdance Day, and each kind of discourse is supported by appropriate stylistic choices of syntax and diction.

There are further sharp contrasts, both of theme and mode of discourse, in the remaining two pieces by the Bread Loaf teachers; they are both autobiographical pieces, but they are no longer directly concerned with classroom relationships, and they present distinct modes of narrative.

The writer of this first piece is herself a Native American; there is in her writing a lyrical quality that distinguishes it and perhaps marks its origin. She is a teacher, and at an earlier point in this piece she records that a substitute was taking her class while she walked on the mountain Ben, the principal of the school, allowed her to go and drove her there, as the paper reports.

Sometimes I walk alone. I have permission from my brother Grant (who we call Johnny) to walk alone on the vision peaks. He is one of the older ones, very traditional. He isn't pleased when I go up. I have to sit with him before. The prayers, he offers them. The cedars, he burns them and washes in the smoke. The days I'm gone, he waits and counts. He shakes his head at me . . .

The first time I went to him, he tried to talk me into staying down. Too cold, too dangerous, bears and ghosts, I'd be too weak to get back off the cliffs . . . its like that. He came at me with one of the sacred numbers and I refused to back down all four times . . . so . . . he had to help me.

He got down the leather bag with the tobacco society designs on it. He keeps 4 or 7 bags on the wall where Linda, his wife and my sister, keeps all of her catholic paraphernalia, interspersed with the school photos of the kids. A sort of holy wall I guess. This bag is a type of parfleche, laced with leather straps. He keeps bundles in all of the bags; this one contains some things from his mother.

He gave me his mother's otter skin. It was a gift to her from her time on the peaks. One of the Little People gave the skin to her. I was told exactly what to say if one of them should come to see me. When I got to the top he taught me to hang it on a lumberpine branch. He took me out along the creek where we tore up some sweet herbs and I carried them up with me. When I got there I arranged the herbs in a circle and always stayed inside it. I also carried some tobacco to use when praying. My fourth item was the rattlesnake rattle my dad gave me years ago.

I'm just a modern walker. I carried my bundle in a backpack, and had a bottle of water. It was late in the day—too late really to be heading out. One of those life crisis kinds of days when I am certain only of needing to walk, up high. Right now. In the end Johnny let Ben give me a ride up the gap.

When Ben dropped me off I stood there wondering about it all. Starting to hear what they had said. I had been spending my energy getting permission to go. What if they were correct? What would come next? The growing soil I was standing on, I might never do again . . .

Throughout an extended narrative her concerns are closely tied to members of her family, to the wild Montana terrain, and to the rituals and customs of her tribe. It is a rich texture for life, firmly held together by strong loyalties—and pursued, as it were, in defiance of alien authorities, cut off from the sources of power, yet possessed of a wisdom and integrity of its own.

And so we come finally to home—or as nearly as we can when it is somebody else's words, somebody else's home. This is a couple of paragraphs from the journal of a South Carolina teacher, written at Bread Loaf:

> What would I have you remember about me? I have nothing remarkable for you. I am a wife, a mother, a teacher. My love for my husband and our two babies *feels* remarkable, though I know love isn't original . . . I write this between changing diapers, answering phones, reading MOO BAA LA LA LA, and helping Steven flush his "poor little fishie" down the toilet. Who am I? I try to be the lover, the wife that a wonderful man needs me to be, to be the best mother I can to these inutterably precious children (our living testament to faith and love), and to be a teacher who truly helps to open up a lifetime of competency and learning for fifty amazingly varied students who have come so expectantly to my English class.
>
> If some deadly accident, coiled and waiting, strikes me tomorrow, remember me as one of millions with dreams and worries, loves and longings, who wants to understand why she must die, and more, why she came to live, and where these miraculous new beings really came from, as I try to juggle my world of diapers, lesson plans, lasagna, neglected friends, postpartum inches, and a bright-haired, brilliant-eyed baby who, after studying the swirling toilet water, can already ask of me, "Poor little fishie died. Where'd he go, Mama?"

This marks a kind of resting point, as though dusk turns to darkness, the storytelling and the speculations come to an end, and if there are any further stories, they will be, in Pilgrim's words, "now I saw in my dream."

The voices from Bread Loaf teachers*—direct or quoted—black, white, Native American—each representing a moment, the still point in a different world. Spot checks of time and place they are, which plot, as it were, changing worlds, trying to interpret them in the process of sharing them with others. By such awareness we extend the environment in which we live our lives—for in talk or in

---

* With grateful acknowledgements to Bob Davis, Mark Hage, Candace Ottertail & Laura Knotts.

writing about our own lives, it is what we make of the world that engages us, rather than what the world has made of us.

Travellers' tales, accounts of experience, our own or other people's, may throw a brilliant light on the generalizations, the arguments that theories construct—and for many of us, it is the stories that outlive the ideas as our guides to action.

Chapter Four

Learning by Numbers

Although it is something that English teachers undertake to do regularly, it is not an easy task to assign a mark, an index of approval, to a piece of original writing. Statisticians favor a method of comparative judgments which are expressed in degrees of "liking": "Which of the following do you like most? Which next?"—and so on down to the item we like least. For a reason I haven't fathomed, such a procedure is called "Q-sort." It was at one time actively applied to creative social products of many kinds—paintings, photographs, poems, etc. Perhaps it was the somewhat dubious sense of objectivity the method imparted that led some experimenters into positivistic statements quite inappropriate to the material under study. Eysenck (1940), for example, seems to claim that he has arrived *at the true order of merit* of a series of short poems. I make this reference simply to indicate that the area of study ought perhaps to be regarded as something of a minefield—or at least a quagmire!

Preference lists, sometimes accompanied by personal explanations of one sort or another, were analyzed by a number of statistical procedures—factor analysis and analysis of variance being the commonest starting points. The assumption here is that a value judgment is a complex of many components. A painting, for example, may appeal to us favorably because it catches the freshness and sparkle of a spring morning; at the same time, it may rate rather low on our space-filling design and proportion. Our final judgment will be a combination of these and other evaluative responses. It is the function of a factor analysis to unravel the value judgments made collectively by a group of judges and reveal the comparative strengths of the principal components. By what is perhaps best regarded as a statistical convention, we shall find that group judgments of value consist of an area of general agreement—that is to say, a common factor—accompanied and qualified by one or more bipolar factors—criterial scales of judgment that may characterize judges by applying either positively or negatively in qualification of their common factor. We have found, for example, that assessments of school-produced writing will yield a fair degree of agreement as a general factor, but that that agreement will be modified by a bipolar factor in which some judges valued the use of colloquial diction as a livener, whereas other judges penalized such usages as misplaced, frivolous.

My first full-scale inquiry using factorial analysis was carried out under the tutorial supervision of Professor Philip Vernon in the years 1948 to 1952. A primary purpose was to seek means of discovering whether secondary school students who were "introduced" to poetry as part of their curriculum showed any tendency to "improve" in their responses; or, in terms of the experiment, to improve in their ability to distinguish poetry that was widely valued and acclaimed from pieces that would be widely rejected as of no poetic merit. Determined not to fall into the trap that had in my opinion snared Eysenck—that of positing a "true" order of excellence in objective terms, irrespective of individual taste, individual perspective—I set out to create a deliberate dichotomy between ordinarily satisfactory poems and what at that time I called "false poems"—pieces manufactured by me under random or extrinsic limitations with the intention to deceive–to look or read like poems, but carry, in the end, no coherent meaning.

The true poems—pieces of less than twenty-four lines by modern writers—were drawn from a larger selection made by me and submitted for preference test to qualified judges. The selection was narrowed to those items on which they showed close agreement and which I judged to represent four categories that had been found in an earlier factorial study (in fact, that of Eysenck): simple, complex, restrained in feeling, abandoned in feeling.

I believe now it was rash—and unnecessary—to label the "false poems" false, since this invokes a distinction that it would be difficult to justify. The truth of the matter is that they were intended to deceive, that they were arrived at by a composition process uniquely different from that ordinarily attempted by a writer; but, that said, what is to distinguish the finished product from the banal or uninspired or otherwise flawed production of a writer of little ability? The dichotomy, then, was represented on the one hand by poetic writing published by accepted writers and appreciated by a general audience of experienced readers, and on the other by fabrications deliberately

aimed at banality, bathos, and/or incomprehensibility. Two true poems represented each of the four subcategories: simple/complex,
abandoned/restrained. For ease of computation the total was set at
fifteen pieces—that is to say, seven fabrications were added and
these aimed at representing simple, complex, abandoned (two in
each), and one restrained piece.

The experiment consisted of presenting these sets of fifteen
pieces to raters and asking them to arrange them in the order of their
preference and, wherever possible, to add a note commenting on
their reasons. On the first occasion, 221 subjects took the test; 18 of
them were accounted "experts"—being English honors graduates
and teachers of poetry; the remainder—non experts—included university students of English, training college students, 18 Services
personnel, and 110 sixth-form pupils—64 taking arts courses and 46
science.

Analysis of the results indicated that the experts as a group
showed a significant preference for the true poems; the whole sample
of 221 raters were significantly influenced by the bipolar factors but
not by their preference for the true poems over the fabrications.
What was notable was the less experienced raters preferred simple
poems, the more experienced preferred complex poems; reactions to
the abandoned/restrained poems tended to be one-sided, overall, in
favor of restraint.

A hundred and twenty of the raters took the test a second time
after an interval of four to six months; their instruction was to rerate
them rather than attempt to recall their previous judgments.

The retest showed a significant increase in the true poem totals,
while response to the fabrications remained, in comparison, little
changed; what change there was seemed to be by gradual displacement as the true poems were promoted. Thus, the findings support
the view that response to a poem tends to take time; we don't
normally respond fully on sight. The poetry we like most continues
to reward us further as we return to it. And by the same token,
response to a poem is likely to be a process of *penetration*: there is,
so to speak, a threshold to be crossed as we move towards a central
understanding.

Caution: Beware of the Fact

Perhaps a word of explanation is needed to make the point that
statistical inquiry may provide evidence of general abilities that do
not yield easily to critical inspection and judgment. Statistical experiments concerning individual opinions do not please the average

statistician because the material counts as "soft data" in their view; and they do not please scholars in the humanities because they appear to discount subjective judgments. The solution, it seems to me, is to ensure that sound critical conclusions are employed to interpret the figures thrown up by the measurements. And if evidence can be found that readers do on the whole improve their responses to poetry as a result of opportunities to read it—and reread it,—that should count as well worthwhile.

At the time of the experiment I recorded these observations on the results of the regrading:

1. All but the least experienced readers tended to suspend judgment upon any item they did not understand—whether a poem or a fabrication. The more complex items (of either kind) clustered about the mean in the first rating, while in the second the true poems, with a few exceptions, moved up, leaving the fabrications behind.

2. Significant changes in mean item scores (i.e.) the average score awarded to a poem or fabrication by all 120 raters) from first to second rating were almost entirely confined to true poems. It was as though the fabrications moved down only by displacement, a rate of change too gradual to show statistically. Thus, in the absence of satisfaction, judgment remained suspended: rejection of an item not obviously worthless was a process of elimination.

3. The main effect observed in the experiment also bears out the need for time to penetrate the experience of a poem. On the second rating the average of individual true poems increased significantly; the raters were better able on the repeated rating to distinguish the true poems from the fabrications.

Scrutiny of the results of the retest by subgroups indicated that first year sixth-formers showed the greatest improvement, with second and third year sixth-formers not far behind. The science sixth-formers stood out for their tendency to prefer the fabrications (though this was less marked at the retest): the boys as a group were remarkable for lack of change. It would appear that improvement in poetic judgment in school depends above all on student/poem contact time. That this assumes the social effects of sharing and discussing views with other readers—fellow students and teachers—must be stressed.

I doubt if there is a real case to make against the claim that the fabrications did in fact merit rejection, whether on sight or after consideration. I don't think meaning can reliably occur by pure accident. The kind of adventitious circumstances—imported to militate against such an accident—were such things as writing by the clock (within the space of a short journey by underground or while waiting for a book to be delivered in the reading room), and by looking around for words or phrases, say from advertisements, to incorporate. It is true that one rater in the experiment believed that my subconscious—in spite of me—spoke to hers: but I could not treat that as a serious objection. Here, at any rate, is a sample of the concocted pieces—one in the category *simple* that could hardly be taken seriously as a work of poetic merit:

Word out of Season

Yours was always the voice I heard
However many spoke beside.
Amid the clattering tongues one word
From you would bring me to your side.

When you were with me all you said
I treasured in my heart, until,
Goodbye being over, in my head
Your precious words were ringing still.

I took your words to bed with me;
For nothing else is mine to keep—
The voice is gone—the mocking words
Destroy my peace, deny me sleep.

And this, in the complex category, simply does not mean anything in the end:

Casualty List

Proud Pharaoh, long from flesh, preserves his dust
In golden pomp; no sacriligious touch
Disturbs his dreams; a thousand years he must
Alone have waited on the perfumed flesh.
Pale silken queens their lonely vigil keep
Bedecked for flattery that none shall pay;
Only the bone remembers; none could weep
For love of lovely dust or moving clay.

Whom the gods love die swift; no burial
Bestows their bones with runes and lingering grief,
"And some there be have no memorial,"
So quick and clean is death. O fate be brief!
All flesh is grass and fiercely burn the fires of war;
No rites of grief shall stay them at the opening door!

Analysis of variance applied to preference ratings by groups of raters in the whole sample of 221 (from sixteen-year-olds to adults) showed this picture: young readers and less experienced readers (e.g.

science sixth-formers) showed significant preference for simple poems; in the arts sixth forms a general preference for complex poems sets in: and the arts undergraduates carry that process a considerable stage further. The most experienced readers of all emerge to a position where a few show significant preference for simple poems and many show significant preference for complex poems.

Perhaps this situation arises because lack of confidence in the value of poetry-as-such results in the younger and less experienced groups being unable to suspend judgment when the complexity of a poem should demand it. To suspend judgment on a poem when it is not understood betokens confidence in the value of poetry in general—and belief in the potential value of the particular poem. When this is lacking, or when it is finally eliminated, an adverse judgment will result.

The intense affinity for complex poetry, with rejection of simple pieces, that characterizes the undergraduate and arts sixth-form groups will be a familiar phenomenon to most teachers. I believe it arises in part because when one is learning to do a difficult thing (whether it is reading more advanced texts or anything else), being successful in doing so is part of the attraction, and maybe one becomes impatient of any task that does not call upon one's powers (Britton, 1954).

Let me add here a few details from a follow-up study that I carried out in 1957 with two fellow-members of the London Association for the Teaching of English, Dorothy Slater and Guy Rogers. A set of eight pieces, four poems by reputable poets and four fabrications—two taken from my previous study and two especially concocted for a juvenile readership—were presented to 800 boys and girls in eight London schools. They were asked to arrange the eight in the order of their preference. The point of the inquiry was to throw some light on the changes in response to poetry that take place during adolescence—in fact, between the ages of thirteen and eighteen. I select three pieces out of the eight that indicate most clearly what we found. The first (here labeled A) is a newly fabricated sentimental piece about a blind man and his dog—sixteen lines, of which the closing four are:

(A)

Now I sit at my cottage door
With my dog at my feet so kind
And though I have no other friend
He'll be good to his master that's blind.

The second (B) is a fabrication from my earlier study—a pseudo love poem entitled *Faithful unto Death*, which begins:

(B)

True love and tragedy go hand in hand.
Consuming passion burns to icy death.
Love's many forfeits make but one demand—
Whatever breathes and loves must pay with death.

Ezra Pound's passionate piece called *Francesca* is (C), which begins

(C)

You came in out of the night
And there were flowers in your hands.

and continues:

I who have seen you amid the primal things
Was angry when they spoke your name
In ordinary places.

The changing views from year to year are indicated here by an index that converts the preference orders into scores (total of plus and minus scores, indicating order above or below the mean: add two and multiply by ten to nearest whole number). The indices are a rough indication of the strength of the age-group responses:

AGE	13+	14+	15+	16+	17+	18+
A. *Blind Man*	40	40	39	37	22	0
B. *Faithful unto Death*	11	14	16	15	16	18
C. *Francesca*	2	9	9	13	24	24

Rejection of the blind man and his dog over the years is dramatically plotted: the relation between the true love poem and the concocted one is more complicated. We suggested at the time that under the strain of emerging into the adult world, the adolescent may need to withdraw into some imagined world: when the strain is great, it may be into the most docile and accessible world that he or she withdraws—a world represented by sentimental values. In matters of emotion, the familiar and safe kind of love—love of animals, pity— may be acceptable when passionate love is too threatening. Of the two love poems, Ezra Pound (C) and the fabrication (B) create very different patterns of response through adolescence, the former being strongly rejected at first and quite firmly embraced by age 17+, whereas the concocted, imitative, blurred expression, being less disturbing, showed far less variation across the age range.

At the time of the experiment, we closed our account with this note:

> Such imagined experience—the stock response, the unoriginal, undisturbing type—gives time to recover balance, but does not itself allow for growth, reintegration, advancement into living. For this we must try to graft genuine poetic experience onto the counterfeit, regarding a taste for the counterfeit in adolescence as the first rung of a ladder rather than the first step to damnation. (Britton, Slater, & Rogers, 1957)

At the time, we were sharply criticized for setting out to deceive the students. Our reply was that this was not a recipe for teaching, but that perhaps what we learned on this one occasion could inform us and give us the patience and understanding that would make us better teachers for the rest of our lives.

The study I undertook with Professor Varnon's help—and that led to the inquiry into evidence of improvement in poetic judgment—began with a more conventional factorial study inspired directly by Eysenck's work. I wanted to see whether a preference test on poems I selected would show the same influences at work on raters as he had found—or would new bases of judgment be revealed. This represents in principle, I believe, a problem to which no definitive answer has been found today.

It was Eysenck's two bipolar factors that were of interest—that distinguishing simple from complex poetry and poems of abandoned feelings from poems of restraining feeling. I chose forty short poems by modern writers in such a way that all were (a) worthwhile and genuine poetry in my opinion, (b) as far as one could estimate, of equal appeal to qualified readers, (c) unfamiliar even to fairly experienced readers, and (d) grave in theme rather than gay. In further search of homogeneity of esteem (the characteristic that favored a weak general factor and hence strong bipolar factors), seven experts arranged these poems in their order of preference. On the basis of their ratings I rejected three poems as being generally preferred to the majority and six for the contrary reason—that they ranked lower than the majority. This left thirty one poems lying within a range of approximately 25 percent of the range of perfect agreement. These poems should thus have been comparatively free to move up and down the scale of preference in accordance with the whims, prejudices, and personal tastes of individual raters.

Twelve more experts (English Honors graduates who taught poetry) were asked to attempt to prepare agreed orders (or "determiners") for Eysenck's two factors—simplicity/complexity and abandon/restraint of feeling: and at the same time to put the items in their order of preference. Twelve non-experts (some more and some less interested in poetry) were then asked to arrange the poems in their order of preference.

The experts found no difficulty in arriving at an agreed order for simplicity/complexity (Reliability Coefficient .939). This was used as a determiner to assist in interpreting any bipolar factors that might arise in a factor analysis of both experts' and non-experts' preference ratings.

The same method was used on the abandon/restraint distinction, but it did not prove possible to arrive at an agreed order of poems for this factor. Nevertheless, plotting the intercorrelations of raters' preference lists did suggest that two groups, or clusters, of opinion existed (i.e., that two factors would be required to account for all judgments).

After inspection of raters' comments and a number of calculations aimed at suggesting interpretation, two bipolar factors were identified: one a clear rediscovery of the simple/complex factor and the other a new factor that distinguished conflict on the one hand from acquiescence or resolution on the other. This was finally established by having experts arrive at an agreed order in response to the following instruction:

> On the one hand, the poetry of conflict, on the other the poetry of resolution and acceptance. It must be stressed that neither of the two views is so crude as to be optimistic or pessimistic in any ordinary sense. In both is present a knowledge of good and ill, delight and pain: in the first the view is dominated by a sense of man's capacity to win the good in a struggle against the odds, or to believe in the good in hostile or discouraging surroundings; in the second it is controlled by a sense of man's capacity to embrace both good and ill, to endure and accept them. (Britton, 1952, p. 121)

The experts achieved a high level of agreement in doing so (Reliability Coefficient of .88).

To illustrate briefly, near the top of the scale—poetry of conflict—was Roy Fuller's poem *The End of a Leave* about the Second World War that begins:

> Out of the damp black night,
> The noise of the locomotives,
> A thousand whispering.
> Sharp-nailed, sinewed, slight

> I meet that alien thing
> Your hand, with all its motives.

and ends:

> Like a hand which mimes
> Love in this anguished station
> Against a whole world's pull. (p. 37)

The poem focuses upon the conflict—a situation that is not final, that must be resisted. And near the bottom of the scale is Robert Grave's poem *Despite and Still*—where the conflicting elements are held in a kind of balance, a resolution (1959, p.4):

> Have you not read
> The words in my head
> And I made part
> Of your own heart?
> We have been such as draw
> The losing straw—
> You of your gentleness
> I of my rashness,
> Both of despair . . .

This agreed order of poems was used as a determiner—a guide as to which of the alternative solutions to accept. The two possible factors were suggested—as I have said—by the way intercorrelations of ratings clustered. If one supposes those intercorrelations to be plotted in two-dimensional space, it will be clear that the values attributed to them could be read off as projections along two orthogonal axes; but when those axes are rotated, a new set of readings will result. It is an accepted statistical procedure to rotate the axes to a position that yields satisfactorily distinct factors with a reasonable number of significant loadings. It was for this purpose that a determiner (or determiners) was plotted on the graph and used as a guide to the meaning of any factors identified. As a result two bipolar factors were identified, the first accounting for 14.6 percent of the variance and constituting a conflict/resolution distinction, and one with 13.4 percent of the variance, which clearly represented the simple/complex factor.

One further question remained that I wanted to ask of the data. The newly identified factor—that of conflict versus resolution—was clearly a distinction at the heart of a poem—something that a superficial acquaintance with the piece was hardly likely to reveal. I proceeded to concoct a determiner for the poems in the test—an order of these same thirty one poems—that represented a bipolar factor with everyday diction and everyday syntax at one pole and specifically poetic diction and syntax at the other (i.e., a scale from everyday language to conventionally poetic language). It seemed to me that these two factors would present—at least approximately— an inside judgment (conflict/resolution) and an outside judgment (everyday language to poetic) on the pieces presented. The outside criterion, for example, placed Louis MacNeice's poem *Entirely* near the top of the order (1959, p. 180):

> If I could get the hang of it entirely
> It would take too long;

And Edith Sitwell's poem, *The Youth with the Red Gold Hair* near the bottom (1945, p. 71):

> The gold-armoured ghost from the Roman road
> Sighed over the wheat
> Hear not the sound and the glamour
> Of my gold armour

It will be recalled that the twelve experts in the group were English Honors graduates and English teachers particularly concerned with poetry, while the remainder were non-experts (they included a psychologist, several science graduates, an economist, a hospital almoner, a bank clerk). Calculating the percentage of variance attributable to each factor, I found that the "outside judgment"—everyday versus poetic language—influenced the non-experts almost twice as strongly as it did the experts (12 percent as against 7 percent of the variance), while the "inside judgment"— poetry of conflict versus poetry of resolution—influenced the experts over twice as strongly as it did the non-experts (18 percent of the variance as against 7 percent) (Britton, 1959, pp. 6-7). I think any evidence, however slight, that understanding poetry is a process of *penetration* could be of value, especially to teachers. That poetry should form part of the classroom environment, giving time for familiarity to grow—perhaps into appreciative understanding, perhaps into passionate addiction—rather than having a poem feature as a showpiece on occasion and then put back into storage—this seem to me crucial, and representative of the way poetry maintains a place, however limited, in our culture.

It must be said that the factors involved in the thirty-one-poem test were likely to be, at least in part, particular to the selection of poems employed—the restriction, for example, to serious rather than light-hearted pieces. Any individual's concept of poems worth investigating is likely to entail bipolar factors (those factors that reflect contrary influences on opinion and so differentiate among judges), and the bipolar factors may at times be peculiar to the particular selection of poems. Moreover, it is a feature of the factor-analysis procedure that a heterogeneous group of people tested by a homogeneous selection of items (poems) is likely to produce one or more comparatively strong bipolar factors. We might, in this context, hazard a guess that changing fashions in poetry (a phenomenon that must have surfaced strongly as readers encountered some of the Georgian verses in the material I have quoted)—changing fashions in poetic style—might produce a bipolar factor contrasting the outgoing with the incoming styles. Such a factor would be likely, I believe, to be uniformly present in a range of studies (Britton, 1953, p. 14).

I have one more experiment to report—a study suggested by the observation that a homogeneous group of persons combined with a heterogeneous test makes for a strong general factor. We should note at the outset that those two terms themselves constitute a scale—a bipolar concept—that any group of persons can only be said to be *more or less* homogeneous and *more or less* heterogeneous *and the same will be true of a selection of poems*. Further, homogeneity in one aspect or characteristic does not entail homogeneity in all other respects. The terms are, therefore, to be taken as comparative rather than absolute classifications.

We can still claim, I believe, that all the analyses of poetic preference anyone had so far, in 1959, reported had used a set of poems carefully selected and reflecting personal values; that was certainly true of the materials I have myself reported in this chapter up to this point. In order to test more rigorously the amount of general agreement possible between judges, I set out (in 1957) to prepare a population—a complete representation—of all the shorter poems (twenty four lines and under) written and published in England since 1900 (not including, however, private commission publishing and magazines). Where applicable, poets were rationed to twenty five poems—so that my list of 4,631 poems (by 200 poets) represents in fact an estimated figure as much as five times that number. From this list I selected (out of a hat) and transcribed ninety three poems; and eleven colleagues and friends who were experts gave them a mark for liking. Their pooled scores gave a Reliability Coefficient of .76, and there were no significant negative intercorrelations. Factor analysis produced a general factor covering 26 percent of the variance and a bipolar factor covering 7 percent. This gives, I believe, a fair indication as to how much general agreement there may be as to what constitutes good, bad, or indifferent poetry when conditions are most favorable: a wide range of poems, randomly selected, produced for publication by writers with varying reputations as poets, and assessed by a number of expert judges, who, while they are experienced readers of poetry over a range of periods and styles, nevertheless bring to bear individual judgments born of shared cultural experience. On average, 67 percent of their opinions are individual responses, 25 percent they hold in common, and a further 7 percent divides them on some minor issue (unidentified).

The obvious next step was to see how far other judges agreed with these experts. For this purpose I chose the thirty one poems out of the ninety three in which the experts showed most agreement. Ten adults of mixed ages and ability, ranging from experts to those whose last experience of poetry was in their school days, indicated their preference orders. Their judgments were analyzed to show a general factor covering 33 percent of the variance and a bipolar factor covering 10 percent. The general factor correlated highly with the experts' ordering; the bipolar factor turned out to be a distinction based on attitudes to changing fashions in poetry— a possibility I referred to earlier. Examination of the poem scores and the comments made with them gave a clear indication along these lines. A group of experts was accordingly asked to prepare an order putting at the top of the list poems that exemplified a late nineteenth-century romantic view of what poetry should be like: serious, earnest, reinforcing a belief that life is all for the best, particularly when Nature is allowed her due role, and beauty, love, piety are revered; poetry as a means of attuning ourselves to the eternal harmony and truth that exist in the universe. And the converse—at the bottom of the scale—poetry that insists on facing the facts, especially if they are ugly or shocking or crude facts; poetry with a mission, not to put us in touch with universal harmony, but to construct out of chaos and meaninglessness something that is in itself significant and satisfying. The experts found no difficulty in producing an order with a high Reliability Coefficient of .92. And this guess at what the second bipolar factor represented proved close to the mark; the resulting order of poems has a loading of .76 in the second factor.

I believe this bipolar factor, unlike others I have described, might arise whenever a broad sweep of poetry is assessed by a group of judges of mixed age and experience of poetry. It reflects, I believe, the pendulum swing by which one generation's enthusiasm tends to be displaced by what the next generation espouses. The period, say sixty years, in which the poems in my test were written—and the people who took part in my enquiries were growing up—saw a change of fashion from the Georgians to Pound and Eliot and the poets of the thirties—and the bipolar factor reflects the living influence of both schools (Britton, 1959).

Looking back at all this from 1990—thirty years on or more—may perhaps enable us to perceive outlines that too close a view of the social and cultural scene today diffuses. Much has changed, of course, but some glimpses of the potential value of poetry to us and the children in our schools may arise from this report on yesterday, its problems and its preoccupations.

Chapter Five

Poetic Discourse
Can you hear what I mean?

So much, over so many years, has been thought and written about the nature of poetic discourse that any approach I make to the topic here must seem heavy-footed, however warily I tread. There is a great temptation, I believe, to strain after the striking, often puzzling, clever comments that scholars and original thinkers have made about what makes poetry precious. Take for example Foucault's comment to the effect that literature "leads language back from grammar to the naked power of speech" (1973, p. 100)—or the claim made by Tzvetan Todorov that "A word's meaning is the sum of its possible relation with other words" (1977, p. 24). But how do we understand and apply such insights? I believe the best way is to begin from the firm basis of what one knows from one's own experience—experience of poetry, of one's own responses to it, and their relation to life as we live it. Such an approach may do no more than provide a framework which, with refinements and additions, carries us as far as we can go; or it may prove its value only by stepping down in favor of newly discovered relationships.

Of course, in speaking about poetry, I realize that I am likely to say things that will in some degree be true also of all literature. How these other forms of literature need to be modified with specific forms of discourse and specific works in mind is a task for later occasions.

I believe poetic discourse presents contemplative reflections upon experience. However, those reflections are not *analytic* in manner; rather, they constitute reflection by re-enactment—or, in the case of imagined experiences or other people's experiences, by a kind of rehearsal that might perhaps be called virtual reenactment.

The important point about reenactment—or contemplation by rehearsal—is that it is an experience held distinct from day-to-day experiences—the material of actual living. (Where that distinction is breached, the virtual experience becomes a kind of hallucination, self-deceptive.) It is from Susanne Langer (1953) that I learned the necessity of distinguishing poetic experience—contemplation by rehearsal—from actual events in which we participate. Referring to the "virtual experience" of a particular poem, she writes: "But nothing can be built up unless the very first words of the poem effect the break with the reader's actual environment" (p. 214). Effecting that break indicates, to me, the taking up of a particular stance towards the experiences represented (or envisioned). Hence the notion of experiences in the spectator role, as distinct from the experiences in which we make decisions and take action—those in which we *participate to effect something in the real world.*

Making that break, taking up that stance towards the text, I believe our response is essentially a response to the *spoken word*, and that has very particular implications. Of course, poets exploit the characteristics of a written language—its visual effect as line is placed relative to line; the effect itself of a line as a separable unit of meaning; the spacing of words on a page—and the physical entity of a book with characteristic appearance, often carefully planned. Nevertheless, it would not be a distortion to call the language of poetry an apotheosis of *speech*. For the truth is that what the reader supplies in interpreting a poem is to a considerable degree a matter of the sounds he or she utters—either vocally or subvocally.

My readers here will be aware that I have found evidence of the importance of those spoken sounds by pursuing the echoes of past readings that can clothe the recollection of a familiar fragment, still carrying aspects of the meaning of the poem from which they are drawn. And it is remarkable how powerful a sense of familiarity may cling to what seem purely structural or grammatical fragments, as evidenced by my struggle to capture half-remembered fragments on that September evening (p. 10).

It should prove an interesting study to discover the means by which a poet will attempt to control the intonations, the logical and emotional precursors of meaning, with which a reader speaks his lines. And, in the end, it must be admitted that his poem will take on different nuances of meaning in your reading as compared with mine. That fact, I think, can only add zest and purpose to the habit of reading and discussing poems together.

What, then, are the poet's resources? I think we have first to recognize that poetic discourse constitutes a multimedia experience. Anyone who recalls the sixties and the era of flower-power will know that multimedia experiences were at that time credited with psychodelic potency—a state of heightened perception and dreamlike relaxation. We have to wonder whether such a state goes any way towards explaining what happens when we are moved by a poem. There is one poet, certainly, who might support the idea. Robert Graves (1949) speaks here of the process of creating a poem: "The nucleus of every poem worthy of the name is rhythmically formed in the poet's mind during a trance-like suspension of his normal habits of thought, by the supra-logical reconciliation of conflicting emotional ideas" (p. 1).

I believe this multimedia nature of the experience offered by a poem is evident to sober common sense when we in fact recognize that a reader's speech is called upon to interpret the meaning of the poet's utterance. By virtue of this simple fact, additional media of expression are recruited, namely:

1. The noises that words make—consonant and vowel sounds. (It is said that Dylan Thomas once replied to a critic of his poetry by claiming that at least it made nice noises—and wasn't that perhaps enough?)

2. Intonation patterns, including pitch levels. (Experiment has shown that poetry in an unfamiliar tongue can convey some types of meaning—the noises that configurations of words make must carry some cross-linguistic, or even universal, significance.)

3. Strength or loudness of voice, and degree of projection. (Radio producers recognize that while an actor may make a good reading of a dramatic poem, he will sometimes ruin a lyric by over-projecting the lines.)

4. Tempo and treatment of pauses. (Archibald MacLeish [1935] springs to mind as a poet who effectively controls speed of reading—from breathless to funereal—by his syntax, rhythms, verse structure, and his use of cohesive links. See for example You, Andrew Marvel (p. 58), beginning:

> And here face down beneath the sun
> And here upon earth's noonward height
> To feel the always coming on
> The always rising of the night . . .

and, in contrast, *Immortal Autumn* (p. 124):

I speak this poem now with grave and level voice
In praise of autumn of the far-horn-winding fall . . .)

5. Rhythmic patterns. (Rhythmic effects in verse have been the subject of many interesting studies—some of which I shall refer to later.)

6. Kinesthetic effects, either overt or internalized. (Awareness of the muscular activities that accompany speech or their shadow effects in silent reading—both are elements that may affect response to a poem.)

But poetic language, as I suggested above, in subtle ways employs the expressive powers of written language as well as those of speech. Some of the effects in verse forms—metric or "free"—will be realized as speech, and others will register as visual effects, shapes on the printed page. Further, since a poem (like any other work of literature) does not by its nature fulfill an immediate communicative purpose and then disappear, the variations in interpretation are more than simply a matter of ways in which your reading would differ from mine, but must reflect wider social and cultural influences upon reading habits and styles from one century to another.

Since meaning in a poem as a whole arises from the way one meaning-bearing element in it interacts with—opposes, supports, modifies, complicates—meaning arising from another source, the guidance afforded by a poet takes primarily the form of a process of *orchestration*—the creation of a text that allows the contributory voices to speak in harmony.

To take a simple example, here is a four-line poem by Edward Thomas:

In Memoriam (Easter, 1915)

The flowers left thick at nightfall in the wood
This Eastertide call into mind the men,
Now far from home, who, with their sweethearts, should
Have gathered them and will do never again.

Perhaps the most striking contribution here is made by the syntax. Closure is suspended throughout three and a half of the four lines in the piece. Those lines constitute a so-called "periodic sentence"—and that effect of "piling up" is followed by the brief lame-sounding clause *and will do never again*. It is lame-sounding by virtue of the substitute verb *will do*—and readers one might expect to know better have criticized that as a weakness—an ending in a whimper. But it is of course the purpose of the poem to stress, not the heroism, not the glory, but the pitiful waste of wartime—reflecting the loss of a generation of young men, the interruption (for some termination) of a way of life for the young; the lame half-line, the withering away of the vitality of the verse serves, surely, to mirror that pitiful waste. Note also that the rhythm of the piece puts a stress on the word *should* in the third line—what might be called the poem's moral imperative.

This is the point at which to pose the question as to how far the rhythmic patterns employed by a poet control the meaning a reader gives to his utterance. It proves to be no easy question as D. W. Harding poses it in his study of *Words into Rhythm* (1976). He regards the discernment of rhythm as an active process on the part of the reader or listener, an "immediate fact of sensory perception" typified by the way we tend to hear the ticking of a clock, not as "tick-tick-tick-tick" but as "tick-tock, tick-tock." It is similarly part of our response to a line of poetry to *rhythmize*—to create a unified sound pattern by reacting to one or more of the verbal elements as salient and subordinating others. In metric verse that process describes our initial response—our reading of the first line we approach: thereafter our rhythmizing has a built-in neuromuscular readiness—a *set* in favor of finding that initial rhythmic pattern repeated. It does not follow, however, that every departure from that muscular set is displeasing to us as poetry readers: what we do find unsatisfactory however, Harding suggests, are lines that fail to conform to the metrical set and yet in doing so achieve no perceptible effect upon the sense or meaning of the passage.

Our question, then, as to how far a rhythmic pattern controls a reader's interpretation receives a cautious answer. Harding insists that speech rhythm, in metrical verse as elsewhere, is "basic and inviolable": a metrical set, once established, may therefore determine which of alternative permissible speech rhythms should be adopted; and where there is a choice of alternative rhythms for the poetic text, the sense of the words will determine which to adopt.

It is interesting to note that, unlike some reputable theorists, Harding does not allow for *modification of accepted speech rhythms* to accommodate to the meter, and seems unwilling to credit any effect of the tension that may exist between the two. Vygotsky (1971), for example, claims that "words resist the metre which attempts to adjust them into a verse" (p. 219) and quotes from a fellow Russian critic: "Rhythm is the interaction of the natural properties of speech components with the rules of composition which cannot be fully applied because of the resistance of the material." A last word from Harding is by way of a warning against fanciful excesses in attributing meaning to rhythmic features—a romantic speciality of some commentators: "All that can be claimed is that the rhythm reinforces—or, very often, slightly qualifies—the sense of the words. Independently of the sense it would have a very limited and uncertain significance" (p. 94).

But—and this is an important rider—the establishment of an emotional stance towards the experiences embodied in a poem is likely to rely considerably upon an effect of the rhythmical form of the verse. And when rhythm embodied in the words on a page is translated into movements or shadow movements of the vocal organs by a reader, it becomes a rhythmic enactment—a disposition of elements of speech that "translates" or transposes the disposition of objects, events or ideas referred to in the poetic text.

Approaching, for example, the edge of a high cliff with the poet in Auden's poem *Look Stranger*, our vocal organs seem to enact the visual effect of pausing and falling that the actual experience could have featured:

> Here at the small field's ending pause
> When the chalk wall falls to the foam and its tall ledges
> Oppose the pluck
> And knock of the tide,
> And the shingle scrambles after the suck-
> -ing surf . . .

F. R. Leavis (1945) comments on this phenomenon in a *Scrutiny* article he called "Imagery and Movement." Quoting from Keats's *Ode on Melancholy* (the line "Or on the wealth of globed peonies"), he comments: "The palpability of "globed"—the word doesn't merely describe, or refer to, the sensation, but gives a tactual image. It is as if one were actually cupping the peony with one's hand" (p. 122). What the poet gives us, then, is "a metaphorical enactment" to which we respond in the act of reading—in "the way the voice is made to move, or feel that it is moving, in a sensitive reading out" (p. 126). Such enactment is, I believe, the equivalent of the way which in speech we suit gesture to our words, and tones of voice to our feelings about what is said. But a page of poetic text has no means of directly representing gesture or tone of voice, and must employ poetic structure in their place.

Metaphorical enactment is probably most directly illustrated in terms of a writer's use of verse structure and line-ending. It is helpful, I believe, to think of a line of verse as a *unit of attention*, each new line signaling—unobtrusively, minimally, so to speak—a fresh start. Given this as the norm, it may enable a poet to enact the existence of a barrier, a fence that has to be surmounted with effort. Leavis goes on to illustrate such a metaphorical move in lines by Donne:

On a huge hill,
Cragged, and steep, truth stands, and hee that will
Reach her, about must, and about must goe:
And what the hill's suddenness resists, winne so.

In the context of the image as a whole—the image of inaccessibility—
the line break between *will* and *reach* presents "an analogical enactment of the reaching" (Leavis, 1945, p. 124). (It is in this way, I think,
that Auden enacts the retreating water and the toppling wavelet when
he breaks the line in the middle of the word: *suck-ing surf.*)

It seems clear that a sensitivity to the operation of metaphorical
enactment will rely heavily upon synaesthetic perception—the ready
recognition of equivalence between one sense mode and another. Add
to this Leavis's insistence that all these effects must be seen within
a broad context—a continuing concerted experience of sense, sound,
imagery, and movement—elements moving in and out of focus as the
poem proceeds, at all stages a multimedia presentation. I am reminded of a thought that has occurred to me often through the years:
If we could employ the descriptive adjective *appropriate*, not in its
usual contingent sense—appropriate *to something*—but in an absolute sense—every element appropriate to every other and to the
whole—then we might have coined a critical term that could usefully
be applied to the nature of a poetic text.

Leavis makes a distinction between "metaphorical enactment" (as
illustrated above) and what we ordinarily term "metaphor". Metaphorical or analogical enactment marks a point at which we might feel
that "imagery" is better called "movement"—though he then goes on
to claim that the subtleties of poetic ordering defy categorization: "The
important thing," he adds, "is to be as aware as possible of the ways in
which life in verse may manifest itself—life, or that vital organization
that makes collections of words poetry." (p. 124). There will certainly
be many and varying occasions where our reading or speaking of a poetic fragment will seem to enact a sequence in parallel to some movement described or referred to in the text.

Turning to metaphor in its broad and usual sense, it is no
exaggeration to claim that our notions of time and space—dimensions of our world schema—are created on a metaphorical principle,
and that these metaphors, once formulated, provide means of ex-
pressing qualitative acts of judgment—moral, social, aesthetic
(up/down, above/below, rising/falling, before/after, near/far,
thick/thin). Metaphor has in fact become a productive resource in the
creation of language. When no accepted term exists for what we want
to refer to, we commonly resort to analogy and use metaphor.

But the fact that in metaphor we *refer without specific indication* leaves the way open for a speaker or writer to make highly speculative references that suggest novel meanings—a device by which poetic discourse might communicate meanings that cannot be encoded in discursive utterance. How, for example, to spell out in plain paraphrase what is implied when Shakespeare has Anthony, face-to-face with the conspirators themselves, address Caesar's body in the words, "Here wast thou bay'd, brave hart!"— an image that conjures up a sense of corporate, ritual cruelty as some kind of disinfestation or exorcism.

Michael Polanyi, with his coauthor Harry Prosch (1975), distinguishes three modes of sign-carried meaning: *indication, symbolization* and *metaphor*. He sees each as representing a *from/to* relationship, that is to say a means of indicating a focal relationship by use of a subsidiary one (comparable with pointing a finger to indicate a required object or direction). *Indication*, then, is the process by which a word or sign is employed in accordance with accepted conventional usage within a culture: calling a spade a spade for example. In indication it is the object (or idea) that is important and focal; the sign itself is not of intrinsic interest and remains in a subsidiary role. This is represented in a simple diagram where "i.i." indicates intrinsic interest, present (+) or absent (-), and "F" indicates focal and "S" indicates subsidiary:

–i.i.   +i.i.

S   ⟶   F

Symbolization represents more than the allocation of a conventional term and relies upon interpretation by both speaker and receiver. Polanyi quotes the example of the use of a national flag; the flag represents our knowledge and sentiments with regard to our country, our experiences and associations related to our nationality. It is these that matter to us—not the flag as a material object. But the flag serves as the focal point that calls up and brings to bear a host of diverse recollections, and it is these experiences, memories, associations that now carry our intrinsic interest. But the diagram needs to find some way of representing this changed form of reference—the process of including, as matters of intrinsic interest, reference to individual personal experiences. Polanyi indicates this by including a recursive loop in the arrow that joins the subsidiary (S) to the focus (F):

+i.i.   –i.i.

S   F

He regards *metaphor* as a special case of symbolization, one that varies in attaching intrinsic interest both to the subsidiary term—the *tenor*, as it has been called—and to the focal term, the *vehicle* of the metaphor. Thus, intrinsic interest attaches both to the verbally formulated analog of what is intended and to the unverbalized meaning, that dependent on the coincidence of individual experience on the part of both sender and receiver. The relation of tenor to vehicle is indicated in the diagram:

t		v
+i.i.		+i.i.
S		F

A simple example may bring out the force of this representation of metaphor. My daughter at about three years of age looked out of the window and saw that after mowing the lawn I had not put away the grass-collector. She turned to me and said, "You've left the hood out". The metaphor—a case of transferring a term for lack of a conventional one—clearly recalled the hood of her pram, still a pretty recent experience for her. But in order to use the word in that way she had to select from recalled experience and apply it to a novel situation: there was a gap to be filled and she filled it by extrapolating from personal experience. And for me to understand what she was saying I had likewise to recall personal experience. The process is thus different from *indication*. It would have been indication if she had used "hood" to refer to her pram—a process of applying an item from her stock of conventionally agreed terms; and while this would of course be associated with her own experience, in using it she would not be called upon to review her experience, select from it appropriately, and transfer it to a novel situation. Finally, intrinsic interest lies in seeing the *hood* as an appropriate image for the grass-collector, and equally in perceiving what I have left lying around after cutting the grass.

I believe this conception of the working of metaphor does in fact describe in a very general way how language functions in a poetic work, indicating how the meaning taken from a poetic work relies upon interpretation by a reader. If, in appreciating the force of a metaphor, we are called upon to fill in the unarticulated term from our own experience, and if, as I believe, a similar reliance upon what the reader contributes is typical more generally of poetic language, then interpretative processes must lead to a variety of effected meanings. Moreover, those meanings are likely to be, in Vygotsky's terms (1962), rich with sense as well as meaning—sense being defined as "the sum of all the psychological events aroused in our consciousness by the word" (p. 146). Perhaps it is this aspect of the difference between poetic text and discursive text that goes to the heart of the matter.

Winifred Nowottny's seminal study, *The Language Poets Use* (1962), sums up much that has been referred to here in her account of *poetic structure*, the mode of organization by which the contributory meaning-bearing elements of a poem achieve coherence and a unity of impression. Poetic structure, she claims, must straddle two extremes; on the one hand, the particularity of concrete detail by which it *realizes experience*, and on the other, the generalizing or universalizing effect by which the poem presents a commentary upon some aspect of the human condition—what she refers to as "a spread of meaningfulness or felt importance of the poem as a whole" (p. 74). This, I believe, is the kind of reading of a poem Jakobson referred to as "simultaneous synthesis" (1972, p. 393)—the ability to "comprehend the entirety of a verbal flow," attending to the sharpness of detail that achieves realization of the texture of experience, while at the same time registering, within the perspective of one's sense of the self-in-the-world—one's world schema—what the view of experience presented implies for that conception. What is required of a poem is that the two dimensions of text—the particularity and the commentary upon existence—should integrate at all points and—finally—speak with one voice.

There is emphasis, then, on the *self-containedness* of a poem; a verbal object is created, which is intimately related to life experiences yet is released, by its isolation, from the movement of events that represent the immediate experience of reality. In this way the poem is able to inspire interpretations that evolve with time and reflect varying environments.

Thus, of the language of a poem it is certainly true, as Georges Gusdorf has said, "the language is not of one but of many; it is *between*. It expresses the relational being of man" (1965, cf. p. 8 in Chapter One above).

Both Leavis and his coeditor, Harding, make prominent reference to the fact that poetry, as a mode of discourse, "creates what it conveys" rather than encoding previously developed ideas. It struck me, with this reference in mind, to wonder whether we knew enough about modes of composing poetry to explore the difference between literary and nonliterary discourse in terms of the inception and composing processes involved.

There are, of course, many accounts of composing processes by poets, but they are richer in personal idiosyncrasies than in interesting and relevant generalizations. I think the important question for me is How does poetry arise?—where does it come from?—rather than matters of "crafting," of successive versions, editing, revising. I remember hearing Robert Frost in some long-ago BBC program declare that "A poem may be worked over once it is in being, but it cannot be worried into being."

I believe the most frequent answer to my question would be to claim that the first step in composing a poem comes in the form of a phrase or group of words—a sentence perhaps—that "occurs", that comes unbidden to mind; that is to say, the process of formulating it is not a conscious one. The words may occur to a mind already contemplating, or emotionally oriented to, the issue that is broached, or they may occupy a mind otherwise idle and desultory. Siegfried Sassoon (1945), for example, records an occasion when "I came to the conclusion that there was nothing for it but to take my useless brain to bed. On my way from the armchair to the door I stood by the writing table. A few words had floated into my head as though from nowhere" (p. 140). And the outcome was a much anthologized poem of the First World War—*Everyone Sang*.

To be sure, it is one of the roles of inner speech to furnish our minds with thoughts or images or stray verbiage, and psychologists have from time to time been concerned to trace sources of some of the serendipitous verbalizations, noting origins in sensations or recollections or half-memories, plucked from the mists of the forgotten past. And a mood of receptiveness to poetry must surely allow for such irrational wanderings, whereas the mental set of logical discourse would tend to smother them.

Harding records two or three cases of writers who make a more unusual claim regarding the origins of a poem. He quotes T. S. Eliot's statement: "I know that a poem, or a passage of a poem, may tend to realize itself first as a particular rhythm before it reaches expression in words, and that this rhythm may bring to birth the idea and the image" (Harding, 1976, p. 86). Similar claims are made, he tells us, by both Paul Valery and Virginia Woolf.

As Harding himself has pointed out, any writer producing metrical verse will proceed to generate words under the influence of the "metrical set" of a rhythm established in the first few lines of a poem; it should not therefore astonish us that control of this kind should begin to operate before words have played any part. We might add that a jazz drummer's skillful performance certainly carries emotive meaning without recourse to words; and there is psychological evidence that internalized rhythms give rise to and control many aspects of normal human behavior. Even young children, Kenneth Lashley (1961) suggests, can take on rhythmic speech in response to what they hear.

Light was thrown upon the mental processes that must enter into the production of discourse when, many years ago, two Soviet psychologists, Luria and Vinogradova carried out their study *The Dynamics of Semantic Systems (1959)*. By an elaborate system of "wiring up" subjects, the experimenters were able to detect what kind of response they made to a series of words read out to them at a slow pace. Ingenious experimental procedures revealed two modes of response; those that associated words in terms of their meaning and those that associated them in terms of their sound—for example, by rhymes, assonances, clang words. Young children habitually responded in terms of the second category; adolescents and adults in accordance with the first, except when they were suffering from fatigue—and then they were liable to revert to association by sound. The experiment clearly suggested the two principal ways in which internal representations of verbal forms were organized into clusters—and the dynamics therefore of their availability to assist our thinking, and hence our composing.

With this evidence in mind, I came to the conclusion that anyone engaged in producing poetic discourse is likely to be listening closely to the sounds of what is written as well as to its meaning—a conclusion born out by abundant experience. A writer's choice of word is rarely, it seems, a fully deliberate process; in Polanyi's terms (1958) it is a tacit process— "in all applications of a formalism to experience there is an indeterminacy involved which must be resolved by the observer on the grounds of unspecifiable criteria: . . . the process of applying language to things is also necessarily unformalized; that it is inarticulate" (p. 81). The writer, in other words, must play the conjuror and take words, as the other takes pennies, out of the air. But the poet, I suggest, practices a double—or even a threefold— readiness, trawling, as it were, three nets in the sea of the subconscious. The first is in search of sense, of meaning; if *morning* were, so to speak the bait, the attraction would be to some such word as *sunshine* or *bird song* or *evening*, but not to *warning, fawning,* or *mourning*. But since in poetry the sound of a word is a vehicle for meaning a second net would be trawling for words associated by sound—associated, that is to say, by the nature of the resulting sound patterning. And a third, perhaps, would be kinesthetic associations related in some way to the articulatory movements that would be involved in speaking the given word—or even to the gestures that might have been by constant habit associated in spoken utterance with the ideas or feelings being presented. This brings us back to suggestions made by Leavis in illustrating "metaphorical enactment" (see p. 59). Shakespeare provides a classic example in the lines spoken by Hamlet to Horatio:

> If thou didst ever hold me in thy heart,
> Absent thee from felicity awhile,
> And in this harsh world draw they breath in pain,
> To tell my story.

What all this suggests is that in the case of a writer of poetic discourse there is more than a triple gain in the chances of discovering meaning—the chances of serendipity. For a word selected for its sound brings with it no predetermined contribution to meaning, but is potentially suggestive of novel meaning; and the same is true of meanings contributed by kinesthetic means.

I can illustrate this with a trivial example of serendipity in a set of verses I wrote some years ago for a BBC Schools poetry program for ten-year-olds. The piece begins—autobiographically perhaps—

> Said an aging schoolmaster, "I'm tired of my school
> And tired of your company.
> I've applied for a permit to live as a hermit
> And that's how I want it to be."

> "Buzz off," said he to the bluebottle fly,
> And "Hop it" he said to the frog.
> At no loss for a word, whatever occurred,
> This prince of a pedagogue.

> "Now make yourselves scarce," he said to the ants,
> As he settled himself on a heap.
> "Skedaddle," he said to the inquisitive squirrel
> That crept from a corner to peep.

> "Be off," said he to the oncoming child,
> And "back" to the forward miss.
> At no loss for a word, whatever occurred—
> A prince of a pedagogue this.

> He muttered and mumbled—we don't know what,
> For he kept it under his hat.
> Alone there he mused till a part of him fused
> With the ground whereon he sat.

> The day grew dark and the night grew cold
> And still in the dark sat he,
> Sighing, "Leave me alone" to the leaves that were blown
> From the boughs of the sycamore tree.

> And they leaved him alone,
> And they leaved him right over.
> And there he lies, buried up to his eyes
> In all the old leaves of October.

As an exercise in puns, I trawled the net for sounds, and the move from "leave me alone" to leaves on the tree was—an unforseen move in the sense that the verb in "leave me alone" constituted another pun when it related to the leaves on a tree. But it was only when this was verbalized that I saw what could be meant by "leaved him alone and leaved him right over"—a sober thought in a light vein that sounded appropriate in the context of a sigh; in short, a suitable way of concluding the piece.

Speaking more generally of my own experience of the composing process, I believe alienation—in the sense of being cut off from familiar associations and personal relationships—creates a need for such expression. I think this is observable both at a major level—the poetry and the personal and expressive writing produced at times of upheaval such as wartime—and at the level of everyday dislocation—the stuff of journeys and excursions, airports and ship voyages, hospitals and prisons. Enforced loneliness, the severance of all the communicative ties with our habitual lives—these must reinforce the unaccustomed blending of wariness with expectation. As T. S. Eliot (1941, p. 12) has put it:

> Here between the hither and further shore
> While time is withdrawn, consider the future
> And the past with an equal mind.

Perhaps the effect is to increase the range of our consciousness, to underline an all-round-looking sensibility, a fusion of past and present, the possible and the actual.

For me, such a disruption occurred fifty years ago during a five-year stint in the signals and radar units of the RAFVR in Egypt, Crete, and the Mediterranean. Unfamiliar people and unfamiliar places—sometimes almost documentary in tone—occupied me together with the fortunes of war, reported, rumored, or witnessed; there's something of each here in what follows.

I was with a radar unit on the edge of the Western Desert for the last few months of 1940, and the whole unit was hustled into Crete on Christmas day of that year. In a village in the northern foothills in early spring of 1941, news came through to us of the fall of mainland Greece to German forces, and I wrote:

Asphodel

Flower of the asphodel
Pale on these southern slopes of Greece;
Flower of the dead
Tall fountain of pale tears,
Queen of the lovely name

Who has no friends.
Men will not touch you.

> They may not remember
> Your dark significance
> But know it is unlucky to pluck you.
>
> Pale on the northern hills of Greece
> Flower the dead.
> This is your season, Asphodel,
> And men who mistrusted you
> Lie low in their homage.

The piece seems to me now strangely detached; it owes more perhaps to echoes of Greek legend about asphodel as a symbol of foreboding than it does to the news of war losses and the advancing German army. Certainly, it is commentary at a safe distance, with nothing of the particularity of experience; life in the beautiful island of Crete might still have been a spring idyll when the news of the fall of Greece came through. Perhaps what is reflected in the poem is a need for assurance—for the unthreatening, for sensibility to values beyond those dominating the present. The poem in this sense might be seen as a process of alienating the present, of denying, at least momentarily, its power over us. Whatever else was written at this time did not survive, unless like that piece they were put in letters home; everything was abandoned when, a month or so later, we left in a hurry before the invading German forces.

At the RAF HQ in Cairo, where I was next posted, life was very different—the teeming energy of a city, comfortable quarters, long hours of desk work in the heat. I wrote this about a year later; the Cairo it reflects is a city of contrasts—in race, in riches and poverty (and in the lively sense for the Western forces that politically and socially we were resented) having been foisted upon the population for our own purposes; no doubt a lucrative source of income but at the same time rowdy, quarrelsome and sometimes cruel.

Boot-Black

> I saw you, off-duty, drinking in a cafe;
> A meek man in a world of masters,
> You sat drinking licorice-water in a Cairo cafe.
>
> That small black head of yours—
> Black lambswool head
> And putty features glistening black.
>
> It was a child's trusting face
> leaned forward from your stooping shoulders,
> Trusting, untrustworthy—
>
> Ill-treated and cruel to your kind,
> All ways exploited, you are
> Cunning and uncomplaining.

You are a million in this small, white, arrogant world.
What shall we do with you? Who is to help you?
What will become of us all?

With the changing fortunes of the war in the Western Desert, Cairo would fill and empty like an hourglass. I wrote a poem that documents for me this feature; the city as a kind of greenroom dedicated to preparing the action that must take place elsewhere.

October 1942

The gharries stand idle in rows, and the streets of Cairo are
   empty.
Oil lamps on the gharries cast light on the lean flanks of the
   horses
And the drivers talk in clusters across the silent street.

Here the clatter of horses hooves and the rowdy shouting,
Last week, of soldiers on leave filled the city,
And the honking of taxis—parked now in darkness, no hope of a
   fare.

A waning moon lights the late streets, painting the silence.

But the paths of the desert are crowded and angry;
Sand-storms in wake of the tanks hide the moon
And are cut by the flashes of guns.

The only lights in the blackout were the oil lamps on the vehicles—the gharries that were usually busy with men and women going to clubs and restaurants. But this night the Services men and women were elsewhere, and the city was strangely silent. Perhaps the poetic structure inevitably reflects the fact that what is realized of the city cannot be matched by any firsthand realization of events in the desert.

Many pieces written in those years reflect more directly the disorientation, the dislocation of normal ties and associations. This on leaving Crete for Cairo in 1941:

For so many of them it is all over now.
Because I am in love
Let me remember that they were in love too
And that there is no real difference between us
Save that I write these words
And there are no words they can write.

I disbelieve the charmed circle that my instincts have taught me;
I have little faith in the human will against bomb splinters,
I know there is no god, nor any gods, to protect me
Therefore I say there is no difference between us,

And loving you Darling, I remember
That for so many of them—and so many of them lovers—
    It is all over now.

And this a year or two later, still in Cairo:

"By the Waters of the Nile I Sat Down and Wept"

It has all been said before, but is felt again
Now, by me, in this place. Reading what they have written
Who in the dirty town long for the clean streets of home
I say it again: accept: we must accept, standing among them

In their squalor and their strangeness;
Prick them and I shall bleed. Wrong them and I will revenge.
To know that, that is my necessity.

We must all of us long for comfort and our own people,
It is a part of us and I accept that too.
But it is not a philosophy.
It is like toothache—and answers no questions.

In the almost fifty years since those events, temporary disorientation has been mainly associated with airports and journeys by air, trains and railway stations. A sense of the dislocation has not been without a welcome shedding of normal responsibilities, and that in itself, I am sure, has contributed to the temporary enlarging of the scope of my consciousness. I think in such circumstances we may take on an all-round-looking sensibility, an openness to the visual and audible evidence of the world around us. Certainly poetry has for me often been the expression of such experiences.

A train journey to Manchester in January 1970 is the occasion for this piece.

A leaden sky and snow heavy on the boughs;
A sameness has fallen over the years
As though events, sharp enough in their passing,
Have merged all into one colourless landscape
This midland scene
As I have known it from time to time—
Five, fifteen, thirty years ago—
Now one.
Today, its point in time,
My purposes and destination,
I hardly know.

A glimpse there of the dislocation in explicit terms, the obscuring of the rules and procedures governing the present. Perhaps the poetic view of experience is always a way of looking that tries to see beneath the conventionally agreed view of people and events to an individual interpretation that strikes a deeper level of significance.

Chapter Six

Imagined Lives

I begin reading a novel rather as though I were setting out to meet someone I haven't met before. I ask questions of the text and am concerned to organize and remember what I learn—or more accurately, perhaps, to speculate, to frame expectations on the basis of what I discover. George Eliot, for example, begins *Middlemarch* by remarking that "Miss Brooke has that kind of beauty which seems to be thrown into relief by poor dress."

Referred to so formally, by her surname, George Eliot seems to be keeping her at a distance. Yet why is her beauty stressed—beauty enough to need no adventitious adornment? If she is the heroine, am I to hear of the unworldly nature, the selflessness of her character? I read on to see: "Her hand and wrist were so finely formed that she could wear sleeves not less bare of style than those in which the Blessed Virgin appeared to Italian painters; and her profile as well as her stature and bearing seemed to gain the more dignity from her plain garments, which by the side of provincial fashion gave her the impressiveness of a fine quotation from the bible—or from one of our elder poets—in a paragraph of today's newspaper."

I learn more perhaps about George Eliot here than I do about the character of Miss Brooke. And now that we are not taken in by the author's disguise and we know that she is a woman, do I find the piece recognizably a feminine—or even feminist—mode of writing? Ought I to adopt a gender-conscious mode of responding?

But wait, the next brief sentence comes down to brass tacks: "She was usually spoken of as being remarkably clever, but with the addition that her sister Celia had more common sense." And with a growing sense of the moral rectitude washing over me—the "Puritan Energy" as the text has it, and the notable beauty of Dorothea Brooke, I move in to meet the company she keeps. I learn that the sisters rejoice in possessing family connections of genteel quality—a quality that the narrator indicates as: "if you inquired backward for a generation or two, you would not find any yard-measuring or parcel-tying forefathers—anything lower than an admiral or a clergyman." No whiff, then, of a market economy. As orphans, I learn, the sisters are living with their sixty-year-old uncle, whose inclination to "let things be" does not meet the approval of his elder niece. Letting things be indicates, I think, an optimistic view of life—moral rectitude will tend to feed on a Jeremiad's perspective.

By the time the first chapter finishes, however, Dorothea's strictures are somewhat mollified for me by her generous affection for her sister, and the relationship between the two has become more complex, less easily predictable. And unpredictability seems typical of the genre to the extent that a novel may be said to raise expectations that it does not proceed to satisfy.

But at this point I should break into the story to recount the special circumstances in which I turned to *Middlemarch* after failing to read it for so long. My reading life has been a long and active one, concerned primarily with texts that deal, practically or theoretically, with the uses of language, both in the home and in schools. I have not been an eager reader of novels, reading for pleasure being more often in my case concerned with poetry, or, for a time, with drama. I did in fact read Tolstoy's *War and Peace* while I was serving overseas in the Second World War—my longest engagement with a novel. But there was a time, a little later, when both critics and friends of mine were active in their praise of George Eliot's *Middlemarch*, and I noted it as something I could look forward to reading when I had a good deal more spare time. That plan persisted, reinforced, as you may imagine, by my need to amplify this account of the uses of language as literature.

I have been interested in the deliberate way the action in Book One of *Middlemarch* develops as the number of characters taking part increases. I meet Dorothea on the first page and the rest of Chapter One is given up to establishing her relations with her sister. Casaubon enters in Chapter Two, but it is only during the last of the parties given by her uncle to celebrate the engagement that we meet the worthies of Middlemarch themselves: Mr. Bulstrode, the banker, Mr. Vincy, the mayor, and the newly arrived young surgeon, Mr. Lydgate (of whom, critics claim, George Eliot tells us a great deal more than we need or wish to know). It is at this party that I learn of the existence of the mayor's daughter, Rosamond Vincy, rated by the worthies at the party as a superior beauty to Dorothea or her sister Celia. Reporting on Lydgate's high opinion of Rosamond, George Eliot steps aside to warn me that "anyone watching keenly the stealthy convergence of human lots sees a slow preparation of effects from one life to another, which tells like a calculated irony on the indifference of the frozen stare with which we look at our unintroduced neighbor. Destiny stands by sarcastic with our *dramatis personae* folded in her hand" (p. 122).

I see this as a commitment on the part of a novelist, or biographer: what fate keeps from me as a participant, and where perhaps society turns a blind eye, it is the storyteller's business to unravel—to show things from a broader perspective.

Expectations and speculations about the married state have certainly played a role in the story so far: I see Dorothea and Casaubon advancing into heartbreak and loathing, Rosamond and Lydgate interested but not yet committed, Mary Garth and harebrained Fred, fond but nothing more—and, away in the background, Bulstrode hiding his plans along with his past history, which his loving wife does not suspect. All this has been broached in the scope of Book One. Speaking of imagined lives, clearly there is already ample material at work in my mind to maintain interest over the rest of the nine hundred pages! Physical beauty, impeccable ancestry, high moral principles—are they enough to rescue Dorothea from the slavery of a disastrous marriage? Is Casaubon to dominate the rest of her life or is there a way out? And what role has the rest of the story for Celia and the abandoned baronet? What will come of the association of Dorothea with Lydgate—is that an escape route for her?

The account of the honeymoon in Rome complicates the marriage theme by introducing Casaubon's cousin, Will Ladislaw, to offer to Dorothea the unselfish adoration that offsets Casaubon's disillusionment and lack of response.

As the story progresses it becomes clear that the man/woman, husband/wife pairs represent, so to speak, tokens in the marriage stakes, the lottery of hopes and frustrations that make up an element in our social existence. Marriages, we are told, are made in heaven; sanctity and the law shore them up. It seems worth declaring that the undertaking has not been adapted to human sentiment and to human frailty. Marriages become, in the West, an index of stability in a paternal society.

It seems clear that Dorothea and Casaubon enter the relationship with inappropriate expectations. She, according to the rector's wife, expected her husband "to see the stars by daylight," and he approached her with "a frigid rhetoric" described somewhat doubtfully as "sincere as the bark of a dog, or the cawing of an amorous rook" (p. 73). As the honeymoon progresses Dorothea meets "some discouragement, some faintness of heart at the new real future which replaces the imaginary"— "gradually changing with the secret motion of a watch-hand from what it had been in her maiden dream" (p. 226), while at the same time it seemed to him that "Dorothea was not only his wife: she was a personification of that shallow world which surrounds the ill-appreciated or desponding author" (p. 223).

The relationship does not improve: Dorothea is committed to playing the part of an obedient and subservient wife, but comes to despise the labyrinthine workings of her husband's studious mind— "having once embarked on your marital voyage, it is impossible not to be aware," the author comments, "that you make no way and that the sea is not within sight—that in fact you are exploring an enclosed basin" (p. 227). Casaubon at the same time nourishes a secret antagonism that is made known only after his death by the terms of his will: Dorothea must forfeit his wealth if she marries Will Ladislaw. It must certainly be reckoned then that the marriage of Dorothea and Casaubon enters the records as one based on false expectations and resulting in failure.

And what of George Eliot? Living with a man who was somebody else's husband and doing so long before women's rights and women's freedom had reached public awareness in the way they have done this century, how did the lives of her imagined creatures rate with her? She seesaws between sympathy and antagonism in her portrayal of Casaubon, while her attitude towards Dorothea seems less critical, more favorable as the marriage relationship worsens. What seemed high-minded morality in our first encounter with her seems to reinforce a sense of her integrity. The failure of her marriage seems to begin to qualify her (as I am sure in reality it has often done) to play something of the role of a marriage guidance counselor.

In contrast, I find the next exemplar of an approach to marriage begin in a happier vein: Rosamond and Lydgate enter by gradual stages into an emotionally charged relationship, which to Lydgate is one of friendship without any commitment of marriage. And Rosamond, whatever her hidden intention, seems for a time to concur. This view of the friendship is for Lydgate a matter of personal and professional integrity. His medical researches are a vital concern for him and an adequate reason for ruling out an early marriage— and his sad memories of a love affair with a French actress who refused to marry him merely reinforces that reluctance. For Rosamond, on the other hand, the friendship seems a welcome flirtation that might always prove susceptible to her own domination and design. The stages by which I am brought to perceive her undeclared intentions are skillfully indicated, almost from their earliest meeting. She was "entirely occupied," George Eliot tells me, "not exactly with Tertius Lydgate as he was in himself, but with his relation to her; and it was excusable in a girl who was accustomed to hear that all men might, could be, or actually were in love with her, to believe at once that Lydgate could be no exception" (p. 196). In the event, it is an unpremeditated emotional response to her that commits him to the relationship she aimed at. When she drops the needlework she is working on, he stoops to pick it up, and raising his eyes to her face he sees in her "a certain helpless quivering"—and at this moment she seemed to him as natural as she had ever been since her childhood. But the omniscient author has already made it clear that what I see happening is Rosamond getting her own way in spite of anything Lydgate desired. She saw his declared intention not to marry in the near future for professional reasons as a resolution she could discount. By degrees, the determination of their relationship passes out of his hands. He bows to "the terrible tenacity of this mild creature" and his words indicate "how far he had traveled from his old dreamland, in which Rosamond Vincy appeared to be that perfect piece of womanhood who would reverence her husband's mind after the fashion of an accomplished mermaid, using her comb and look-ing-glass and singing her song for the relaxation of his adorned wisdom alone" (p. 628).

With what subtlety the errors of Dorothea's marriage to Casau-bon are complemented and inverted by the cross-gender relation-ships that bind Lydgate to Rosamond! Straight is the gate and narrow the way that leads to righteousness—or to a happy marriage. Some responsibility for the failed marriages must go to Dorothea and Lydgate, but there can be no doubt that the deviousness that moved Casaubon into revenge has more in common with the terrible tenac-ity by which Rosamond overcame Lydgate.

It is Lydgate's decision that the certainty that Rosamond will never love him is an easier thing for him to bear than the fear that he will cease to love her. I am reminded that Freudian psychology marks the point in adolescence at which a dominant need to be loved usually gives way to a supreme need to love. Lydgate foresees the dreariness of their life together; "it was inevitable that . . . he should think of her as if she were an animal of another and feebler species. Nevertheless she had mastered him" (p. 719). And Rosamond "was in such entire disgust with her husband that she wished that she had never seen him" (p. 716).

I recall that George Eliot threw out a hint, that we could not ignore the relationship that linked Lydgate and Dorothea. When he

was summoned to attend Casaubon, he made a point of speaking to
Dorothea, warning her that her husband's disease was one that
might worsen rapidly. It was as he was leaving her that she said,
"with a sob in her voice—'Oh, you are a wise man, are you not? You
know all about life and death. Advise me. Think what I can do. He
has been labouring all his life and looking forward. He minds about
nothing else . . . .' " For years after, Lydgate remembered the impression produced on him by this involuntary appeal—this cry from soul
to soul . . . (p. 324).

We sense in this a flash of that moral rectitude in Dorothea that
survived even the misery and emptiness of their life together—and
I am led to conclude that Lydgate realized it. There is the dawning
here of the honesty and integrity that link the two characters and
that goes on to play a substantial role in the recovery of Lydgate's
reputation in Middlemarch—and even tackles the cause of his failure in marriage. My anticipation at this stage in the story leads me
to contemplate the possibility that Dorothea, given a further opportunity, might indeed make a successful marriage with Lydgate before
the novel ends. As events turn out, however (matchmaking on the
part of a reader is a risky undertaking!), Lydgate and Rosamond
present the second of the husband-to-wife relationships portrayed,
that of the wife whose selfishness, deviousness, and tenacity of
purpose dominate the union and deny any possibility of shared
happiness; and of the well-meaning husband whose conception of a
wife's role seems to go no further than that of the adoring lover and
mistress of the household.

Dorothea's visits to Rosamond provide further observations upon
marriage. Dorothea declares that "there is something even awful in
the nearness it brings" so that an extramarital affair murders our
marriage,"and then the marriage stays with us like a murder—and
everything else has gone."

I must wonder how far this view represents the perspective of
the character, and how far that of the author. It must have been a
much more widely accepted view in the society of the 1830s than it
would be today; from the era of the first contraceptives, the liberation
of the adolescent after the Second World War, the increase in divorce
and remarriage, and accelerated growth of joblessness, and now the
onset of AIDS—much has altered, in one direction or another, the
status of marriage in contemporary society. Living on through a
"murdered marriage" must in Western society today be a much rarer
misfortune than chronic unemployment or homelessness. And it
must be one of the advantages offered by the novel as genre that we
may try to contemplate and understand what effects attend the
passage of time.

The third prototype of marriage, in my interpretation of *Middle-march* is that of Bulstrode, the banker, and his wife Harriet. Dorothea could hardly complain of the awful nearness of that union; their isolation, their estrangement, seems to have been of long standing. Earlier references to Harriet's role suggest that she takes for granted his professed holiness—believes in fact that "he was one of those men whose memoirs should be written when they died" (p. 382). She is prepared to stand up to her brother, Mayor Vincy, deploring the way he has spoiled his daughter, Rosamond, but gets little response from her husband when she tries to interest him in Lydgate and his marriage to Rosamond.

When the news breaks regarding Bulstrode's past, Harriet takes time to come to terms, alone, with the fact of his duplicity, his hidden and shameful past, the superficiality of the piety he professes. Like Jacob in the Bible story who wrestled with God, she struggled with the demands fate made of her—and arrived at a resolution by which she could return to her husband and offer him comfort. " 'Look up, Nicholas.' He raised his eyes with a little start and looked at her half amazed for a moment; her pale face, her changed, mourning dress, the trembling about her mouth, all said, "I know"; and her hands and eyes rested gently on him. He burst out crying and they cried together, she sitting at his side.... She could not say, 'How much is only slander and false suspicion?' and he did not say, 'I am innocent' " (p. 808).

I can't help thinking of the early schoolboy experiments in which I played with magnets when I read of the to-ing and fro-ing, the misjudgments and suspicions, the doubting and disapproving that kept Dorothea and Will Ladislaw apart until, finally, like two magnetic poles they came firmly together as they had to do. I find the reconciliation beautifully managed and moving. It affords Dorothea the role of benefactor and seeker after (comparative) poverty; but their subsequent life moves out of the story's focus. Even Dorothea herself describes the match a little disparagingly; she reports to Celia, "I might have done something better, if I had been better. But that is what I am going to do. I have promised to marry Mr. Ladislaw; and I am going to marry him" (p. 880).

What am I to make of the fact that the story ends with an account of the idyllic and at the same time unremarkable story of Mary Garth's marriage to Fred Vincy? Dorothea declares on one occasion, "I am fond of knowing something about the people I live among", and no doubt this speaks also for George Eliot herself. And in a tapestry that unites the baronets and the clergy, the doctors and the local dignitaries, the tradesmen and the villains, her last illustration of married happiness goes to the common people, and to ordinary expectations of a good life.

The worthies of Middlemarch, we are told in George Eliot's "Finale," spoke of Dorothea to their young ones as "a fine girl who married a sickly clergyman, old enough to be her grandfather," and little more than a year after he died, married his cousin, "young enough to have been his son, with no property, and not well-born" (p. 896). But to this she adds her last word on Dorothea; "The effect of her being on those around her was incalculably diffusive; for the growing good of the world is partly dependent on unhistoric acts; and that things are not so ill with you and me as they might have been, is half owing to the number who lived faithfully a hidden life, and rest in unvisited tombs." (p. 896).

I might well close my account of *Middlemarch* by recalling it as a story in which "Destiny stands by sarcastic with our *dramatis personae* folded in her hand" (p. 122). So much change, so much uncertainty across so many levels of human society within a diverse local group, comes at last to rest.

The surprises, the disappointments, even the passionate assurances, did not seem alien to me—have in fact reinforced a sense of life as we live it, accelerated at times and lagging at others; embracing areas of satisfaction amongst frets and annoyances, linking my satisfactions and disappointments with the eventfulness of other people's experiences—but, above all, controlled by George Eliot's unusual intelligence in the narration.

I guess life stories are for the novelist a Joanna Southcott's box. Our expectations are kept alive by the very failure to foreclose. I refer in the final chapter of this book to Vygotsky's idea that it is the purpose of a work in the verbal arts to offer an opposition to the anticipated judgments of a reader concerning the events narrated. Work by M. M. Bakhtin, produced in Russia over a period in the twenties and thirties of this century, and only recently translated into English, confirms my notion of the pleasure I find in responding to such "reversals" when I read an extended and complex narrative such as *Middlemarch*. In a recent critical account, Saul Morson (1991) discounts the attempts many critics have made to identify Bakhtin's view of literature with widely diverse theoretical perspectives and comes down firmly on the unique value of the novel as "the best way to communicate a vision of people as freely responding to complex specific situations" (p. 208). What Bakhtin's claim amounts to, it seems to me, is that the novel should be seen as the outcome of dialogue between a creative writer and a creative reader, and that, as such, it can communicate a meaning that discourse according to rules—whatever the source or nature of the rules—cannot match and cannot explain. Bakhtin's best known work—certainly in the view of his native Russian readers—was his commentary on Dostoevsky's novels. Morson considers that Bakhtin "came to regard the novel—the great realist novel of Dostoevsky, George Eliot, Goethe, and Tolstoy—as the supreme achievement of Western thought because the novel, more than any other literary or nonliterary form, respects the particularity of context, the eventness of events, and the uniqueness of personality" (p. 208).

In the first of the four essays that make up *The Dialogic Imagination* (1981), Bakhtin sets about to mark the distinction between epic, representing one of the early established genres, and the novel, as the only genre to be set up after writing had become an established mode in most languages. He has a great deal to say about the difference that entails.

> By its very nature, the epic world of the absolute past is inaccessible to personal experience . . . One cannot glimpse it, grope for it, touch it; one cannot look at it from just any point of view; it is impossible to experience it, analyze it, take it apart, penetrate its core. It is given solely as tradition, sacred and sacrosanct, evaluated in the same way by all and demanding a pious attitude toward itself.
>
> (p. 16)

Speaking the voice of the past is to enter a closed world that cannot adapt to the changing needs and desires of an age it is unable to response to, and people whose freedom is as yet unexplored. Crucial in the case of the novel is the fact that its language is the voice of the present in all its openness, its incompleteness, its indeterminacy. "The novelist is drawn towards everything that is not yet completed" (p. 27), and it is this inconclusiveness that gives the genre its vigour. Moreover, the older genres, such as the epic, have been influenced in that same direction; Bakhtin speaks of their *novelization*—their emergence into contemporaneous treatment as aspects of living existence in all its uncertainty. Thus is extended the range of uses of language to explore and assert my own experience of the nature and necessity of human relationships.

Bakhtin comments on the means by which this freedom was gained; it happens as a consequence, he believes, of the general tendency to counter habits of solemnity and reverence with laughter—to seek relief by mocking sacred objects and sacred observances. The solemnity with which the past was preserved in the epic would have, in human nature, its counterpart in fun-making and mockery, and this prepared the way for the older genres to learn to speak the language of the imagined and inconclusive present. In short, novelisation extended to the older arts the chance to *play*—to remake the world just as every generation of children may do in their make-believe constructions, their fantasies, if they are given the opportunity. Bakhtin points out that it is only through the novel that we have the possibility of "an authentically objective portrayal of the past as the past" (p. 29). It is when the past is treated as a part of the "world-in-the-making" that it is able to take on, however distant in time, something of the incompleteness, the openness to change that marks our sense of the present.

Since the novel treats of life as it is lived, the author may become a part of the story, and this may involve changing relationships between fiction and nonfiction. Since the novel is in the vanguard where change is concerned, it may be seen to indicate ways in which literature as a whole will develop. Its orientation will be not to the past, but to an open, uncertain, and challenging future—a future in which human freedom may prosper.

Bakhtin relates the new concepts associated with the novel to the changing role of language in society; the world, he says, "becomes polyglot, once and for all and irreversibly" (p. 12). Every novel is, as it were, a concert of voices in collaboration. The author must play the conductor but will draw upon what other voices have originated; hence the role of the dialogic imagination. Individual freedom is shared freedom—shared within the culture of a social group, the source of its power but also of its boundaries.

Morson is convinced that Bakhtin not only does not subscribe to any current theoretical account of the role of literature, but has in fact little use for the ability of our language to handle generalizations. Over against logical deduction, for instance, and other examples of what he labels "theoreticism," Bakhtin valued "surprisingness" (Morson, p. 204). Taxonomies will always, by this view, tend to limit the freedom of thought of those who subscribe to them. All the -isms, the great theories, tend to ignore the fact that what "in human life usually contains the soul of activity and the meaning of event, lies precisely in what cannot be transformed into rules or generalities" (p. 206). For Bakhtin, as for Morson himself, literature exists as a means of recording and contemplating whatever it is that makes our lives uniquely our own and unrepeatable, part of the network of relations that make up a society.

In such a manner, George Eliot exercises my freedom, since in threading the tangled web of relations that reconstruct the society of Middlemarch, I contemplate my understanding of marriage as a social institution and an individual predicament, and in countless other ways respond to and participate in the particulars of individual lives lived long ago.

Chapter Seven

Literature in Its Place

I began, in Chapter One, to speak of the "anatomy of human experience," and I traced its beginning in the early interaction of a child with an adult, arriving at common understandings before speech could communicate them. And then, in the course of months, the interchange of meanings becomes possible, all in enacted make-believe play.

Michael Oakeshott writes in *The Voice of Poetry in the Conversation of Mankind* (1959) that voice can be recovered by any of us who can recall our first uses of speech in infancy. "Everybody's young days," he tells us, "are a dream, a delightful insanity, a miraculous confusion of poetry and practical activity in which nothing has a fixed shape and nothing has a fixed price . . . . We speak an heroic language of our own invention, not merely because we are incompetent in our handling of symbols, but because we are moved not by the desire to communicate but by the delight of utterance" (p. 61).

The delight of utterance certainly brings to mind my younger grandchild as she was a few years ago. You see her here at twenty-two months of age, talking with her mother, Alison, and my wife (whom she knows as Danny):

A: (to Lucy) What's your name?

L: Kathy.

D: Katherine?

A: Is it really Kathy?

L: No

81

A: What's your name really?

L: Sheila

A: It's *not* Sheila! What's your real name?

L: Lucy.

A: Yes!

D: What's mummy's name—do you know that?

L: Yes. Chocolate!

A: Chocolate? I'm not called chocolate. What's my name? What's mummy's name?

L: Alison.

At twenty-two months, trying out the possibles—alternatives to the actual—must be delightful; but very soon more fully imagined alternatives will constitute the delight of utterance as Oakeshott understood it. Lucy approaches that when, two and a half years later, she begins, very properly, "Once upon a time there was a little dog called Lucy . . . and . . . he won and they went into a dairy and there they had a nice time . . . ." (I suppose the "word that means me" must acquire a very special significance to a child—the word that the keepers of the child's world may utter in praise or blame, to love or to reject—and that one can hardly expect a sensible child to hear dispassionately.)

Lucy was not a great storyteller; her interests seemed at this stage to be in how things *worked*—what made them tick, what you could *do* with them. It was Laurie, my elder granddaughter, who explored the whole range of what is possible when delight of utterance takes precedence over the informative function. Take, for instance, the language of her make-believe situation at the age of four years one month as quoted in Chapter One. She is playing the role of mother and I am her child: "Now its time for the little darlings to go to sleep," she begins; and after a suitable pause she ends with, "Morning!" A couple of months later, we have the encounter recorded in Chapter Two in which Laurie plays a concert of roles—impersonations of authoritative figures in a succession of scenes, "I'm the mummy," "I'm the school teacher," "Now I've got to be your mummy coming home."

This first enactive, imaginative mode of speech is certainly something we may often observe. I see three- or four-year-olds walking down the street, leaning outwards from their grasp of an adult's hand and doing what I can only call "holding forth." That they should be encouraged to do so by the way we listen and respond seems to me crucial, a way of sharing their lifespace and the role that language plays in their early experience. It's likely that at this early age children find it easier to manipulate verbal responses to experience than they do to adapt their behavior in relation to the people and objects that feature in their environment.

It seems to me important to realize that the language in which we make these verbal responses establishes the mode in which, throughout our lives, in talk, in reading and writing, we engage with the imagined experiences offered to us in literature.

When Michael Oakeshott wrote of the voice of poetry in the conversation of mankind, he made it clear that that voice must cover imaginative constructions—not only those of poets, but those of writers whose purposes were, broadly speaking, literary, and also works of art produced by painters, potters, sculptors, and other creative makers. That same breadth of purpose marks what Vygotsky wrote of in *The Psychology of Art*. While his illustrative examples are all taken from the verbal arts, he makes references from time to time to other symbolic modes. He stresses above all the educative purposes of art: "From the most ancient times art has always been regarded as a means of education, that is, as a long range program for changing our behavior and our organism" (1971, p. 253). The effects of art take their time; they are no quick fix. Vygotsky calls it a delayed reaction: indeed, "Art is the organization of our future behavior. It is a requirement that may never be fulfilled but that forces us to strive beyond our life toward all that lies beyond it." (1971, p. 253). It is, I think, a mistaken pragmatism that underrates the effect of a dream or a vision upon our sense of reality.

The language of literature, Vygotsky suggests, represents the merging of conscious and subconscious processes. "In our minds there exists a continuous, lively and dynamic connection between the two areas"—and this is recognizable both in the language of literature and in the language of children's make-believe play.

It follows that works of art enable subconscious processes to be given social expression, and by this means contribute to the mores of our society. He suggests that the rhetorical means by which this is achieved is in setting up formal constraints that modify the anticipated effects of the content—the events narrated. "The form," he suggests, "is not a shell which covers the substance. On the contrary, it is an active principle by which the material is processed and, occasionally, overcome in its most involved, but also most elementary properties" (pp. 145–6). A plain, unvarnished factual account of events might, for example, be frightening to a listener; on the other hand, the way the story is told might so underplay the fearful aspects—its "elementary properties"—that the whole situation no longer seems threatening

The example Vygotsky gives of such a reversal refers to a short story by the Russian writer Bunin; the material consists of the association between a young woman student and a guards officer. It is an account of an infatuation that ends in the girl's suicide. But the form in which the story is told—its round-aboutness, its broken-time sequences, its omissions—"processes the material," softening, sweetening its effect. It might be helpful to think of the way the musical form of a song will differ from the grammatical structures of the words that are sung. The difference lies in the ends or purposes of the music. Whereas the meaning of the words might be seen as a straight line from unfamiliarity to familiarity, from ignorance to understanding, the form of the song, Vygotsky suggests, "can be graphically represented as a curve around a straight line" (p. 148). The author sets it out in his way, Vygotsky says, in order to "undo life's turbidity and transform it into a crystal transparency. He did this to make life's events unreal, to transform water into wine, as always happens in any real work of art" (p. 154).

We certainly expect of a work of literature that it will embody an evaluation of experience and will not merely record the circumstances, the events and encounters of life as we live it. The culture of any society consists in the evolving accumulation of such evaluations. In Vygotsky's account, effective form is a constant; the reversal, in a full sense (as he applied it to Bunin's short story), will be occasional and not universal. A work of literature may indeed distill the truth of a general sentiment—something of the "all in each of everyman," as Coleridge has it. It is by means of the individual responses, whether to the events of our lives or to works of art—and art-like works—that cultural mores are determined. Vygotsky for that reason believes that any explanation of the nature of responses must begin by tackling the problem areas of *emotion* and *imagination*.

He does so himself in his final work, *Thought and Language*, published only after his death. The book was suppressed two years later and remained so for twenty years. It is in this book that he states his belief that *intellect* and *emotion* must be seen in close relation to each other. This is a view that we as teachers learned from I. A. Richards, *How to Read a Page (1942)*. Richards suggests that a reader's mind should focus on "awareness of interdependence . . . to see that our sense of the hanging together allows no severance of head and heart—no neutral intellect fighting against the motives which make up its activity" (p. 240). Similarly, for Vygotsky, intellect and emotion meet at the immediate level of word meaning. Analysis, he believes, "demonstrates the existence of a dynamic system of meaning in which the affective and the intellectual unite. It shows that every idea contains a transmuted affective attitude towards the bit of reality to which it refers" (1962, p. 8). The expression of any idea, that is to say, has in it an element that represents the way we feel about it.

An individual's ability to handle word meanings is thus seen to be an index of personality that throws light upon intellectual, social, and affective characteristics. *Thought and Language* examines the ways in which an individual child sets about developing the use of word meanings that reflect the understandings of adult members of the community into which he is born. Vygotsky concludes that thought and language "reflect reality in a way different from perception" and form the "Key to the nature of human consciousness." "Words play a central part not only in the development of thought but in the historical growth of consciousness as a whole. A word is a microcosm of human consciousness" (p. 153).

The words we have used in speaking, in writing, in thinking about the world we live in, present an ordered awareness as close to the truth of our existence as we can master. Learning to use word meanings in ways current among adults in a society is a process that takes time—and may in fact never be satisfactorily achieved by many of its members. Progress depends on building stage by stage. A striking early example of this fact relates to the power of *imagination*. At the earliest stage, children must rehearse in active play the scene that strikes their fancy; if they do not enact—rehearse perhaps—a make-believe performance, there is no imagined construction. But at a later stage, make-believe play that is rehearsed in the mind, make-believe without action, becomes possible—and the power of imagination is born (Vygotsky, 1978, p. 93).

In his work on the psychology of art, Vygotsky illustrated broad general concerns, but with a focus upon fable, short story and tragedy. In earlier chapters, I have referred to narrative—spoken and written—enactment and drama, argument, poetry and novels; and using the term loosely, I have included all of these save argument under the name of *literature*. The term is one we are used to in many contexts—from its early appearance relating to folk tales and fairy tales, through leisure reading at all stages, to examination work in high school, and through to a major role in academia, where it is often given one of a wide range of particular, and sometimes even contradictory, definitions.

The forms of writing, reading, and talking that make up the material of this study have been somewhat scantily perhaps, defined as utterances in the role of spectator. Pages 28 and 29 of Chapter Three provide a formal description. Its everyday uses take the form of familiar chat—exchanging views and news—about the weather, about our states of body and mind, about neighbors, family, friends. But there is always something more than just information in our words uttered as spectators. There is always in some degree an indication of how we feel about someone or something; our words carry, as we have said, the pluses and minuses of our verdicts upon the world. They share characteristics of works of art as Vygotsky defined them: they have aesthetic value—they may be either works of art or, at a less intense or finished level, they might be called art-like. But as we know, it takes a writer and a reader to constitute a work in the verbal arts—and anything we offer in this way has a putative existence.

Focussing on what is offered—and I am thinking at the moment principally of something written by a child—what is offered has what might be seen as an inbuilt *direction*. It is likely to be going somewhere, because the writer's approval of her/his own work goes with it, and we learn from experience that what satisfies him/her today is likely to lead to further demands the next time. This is a movement of change by which a writer builds a highway of past satisfactions. And the message for us as teachers is that we should not discourage early enthusiasms because they are art-like in what may seem to us crude ways. It is up to us to recall that they travel the road we ourselves set out upon.

The treatment of works of literature that originates in the universities, but permeates activities at many levels, is governed by the concept of the literary canon. Every new work submits to the process of seeking a place in that hierarchy; and old works are maneuvered up or down in the order as opinions change with regard to them. Of course, individual likes and dislikes obtain, but there is also a sense in which a fairly reliable social order also exists. It will fluctuate as works gain or lose esteem and it will show variations from social group to social group, but recognition of the standing of particular works is likely to be some part of the social and academic context in which they are regarded and discussed. My argument here is that no such place-seeking and place-holding procedure need limit the movements of change open to spectator-role artifacts; we like what we like, and that may at one and the same time include a Shakespeare sonnet, a limerick, a current magazine story, a best-selling novel—meeting different aspects of our immediate concerns without setting up in competition.

Such a view finds strong support among critics who fight for adequate recognition of women writers and working-class writers. The authors of *Re-Writing English: Cultural Politics of Gender and Class* (Janet Batsleer, Tony Davis, Rebecca O'Rourke & Chris Weedon, 1985) claim that the literary canon consists not simply of a series of recommendations but of a hierarchy "whose value derives not from any intrinsic properties but from the fact that they necessitate a continuous process of comparative placing and opposition" (p. 29). The ordering of a "literary ideology" becomes the basis of grades in school examinations, in degree results, and in the career possibilities open to academics. F. R. Leavis and his fellow writers in *Scrutiny* are seen as prime upholders of the literary checklist and condemned for their elitism and their intolerance of what they judge as "mass civilization." On the other hand, the Schools Council, sponsored by the Ministry of Education, appears to the writers of *Re-Writing English* as useful in loosening the stranglehold of the university-based schools examinations boards and so creating freedom to experiment in the curricula of some state schools. What is recommended by these critics is then a much broader conception of what is suitable reading matter in high schools and what kinds of writing should be encouraged—and clearly this includes much greater tolerance for expressive and conversational styles.

American concerns in this field focus more directly on awareness of gender, whether in the student, the teacher or the writer. In an essay on "Gender Issues in the Teaching of Writing" (1992) Nancy McCracken sets up distinctions between what is essentially "masculine" and what is essentially "feminine" in conception, while she is careful not to attribute either role to a person. She cites evidence showing how classroom discussion relies mainly on contributions from boys, in part, no doubt, because there are strong cultural pressures against women's voices being heard too frequently. Masculine talk is seen as speaking in order to *be right*—to put someone else in the wrong—"machine-gun language" (p. 170) it has been called. A women's role in life is seen as that of nurturer—and this suggests that women are likely to find greater difficulty in acquiring the "academic goals of rationality, critical thinking and autonomy." (p. 171). Educators must find ways of helping women to apply their "central ways of knowing—care, concern, connection." (p. 171).

McCracken quotes sociolinguistic accounts of differences observed between men and women in their modes of conversing: when men talk together they handle mainly safe, public topics and proceed in a kind of one-upmanship rivalry. When women talk, they tend to deal with unresolved, open and often private topics, and they do so by collaborative inquiry (p. 173).

Applying such observations to the teaching of writing, McCracken believes that students would profit by keeping a journal in which they share their concerns with fellow students. She stresses the need to encourage use of a range of models beyond the customary critical or expository essay; women's ways of thinking find expression in a wide variety of forms and represent powerful alternative modes of intellect. She concludes that "where we listened only for major and minor premises, we must now listen also for truth statements shaped into different patterns, e.g., metaphors and parallel narratives," and she names the "non-academic, but central, modes of Celebration, Lament, and Puzzlement." (p. 180).

In a further essay, "Re-gendering the Reading of Literature," McCracken wants us to see that school reading has mostly been defined by what boys do, and this has been mistakenly established as the sole reading position allowed to girls. This is necessary, she says, because both girls and boys grow up reading as boys. Until recent years the stories read in schools have largely been the work of male writers, and most of us have modeled our reading habits upon the critical approaches expected of men. While stories by women have become more plentiful in books and magazines, English teachers brought up in University schools dedicated to the literary canon find themselves in difficulty when faced with new works in unfamiliar modes. They need to make a fresh approach to these texts, subordinating all they learned in academic circles about ways of treating the eternal themes to the conclusions arrived at by shared reading and discussion. And in such discussions, what we have learned from experience, both our cognitive responses to events and the tacit dimensions of our beliefs and expectations are the final arbiters that control the conclusion. I think we should remind ourselves of Keats's definition of "negative capability" in a letter to his brother and sister-in-law (December 21, 1817): "that is, when a man is capable of being in uncertainties, mysteries, doubts, without any irritable reaching after fact and reason." The way it feels to the reader, what it does for him/her may yield a more lasting influence than any critical analysis aimed at advocating what is often regarded as an expert interpretation.

Where the exercise of the imagination is concerned, we may well ask what agency can claim the right to oversee individual preferences. Politicians of all parties, authoritarian powers in education, in industry, in society at large, may claim such a right and annex the power to enforce it; and the more unequal a society is in the distribution of its wealth, its resources, and its employment opportunities, the greater will be the constraints upon the imaginative activities within the society at large. The "conversation of mankind" that Oakeshott envisaged was a free exchange of many voices, and prominent among them were the voices of poetry, the "delight of utterance."

It seems to me that what above all else is required in education is that girls and boys, men and women, who have learned to read in men's ways, should learn to read also in women's ways—open to the demands of caring and connecting, of playing the believing game as they approach possible new sources of imagined or recorded experience. McCracken concludes her chapter by saying: "Only as we add literature written from multiple perspectives and teach ourselves and our students to read as both men and women will we start to reap the individual and cultural benefits long attributed to the reading of literature" (p. 20).

I envisage a mode of reading that promotes "care, concern, and connection"—one that could become a central mode of response to spectator-role offerings throughout the range from fairy stories to Shakespeare and the whole academically accepted literature, including the kind of children's offerings that form stepping stones on the high road of their imaginative satisfactions—a highroad that stretches the length of a lifetime.

And that brings me to the end of this particular journey; I finish it in the company of Laurie, my elder grandchild. A week or two after her fourteenth birthday I asked her to come and talk with me about what she liked to read, a matter which I had previously had no opportunity to discuss directly with her. The record of our conversation was the last thing to go into the transcript.

Laurie has featured in my earlier chapters as my elder grandchild, but you need to know that both she and Lucy spend half their time with Alison, their mother, and half with their father, and in that family they have three half-sisters. Laurie has this in mind in what follows:

L: Well, recently I've been reading a crime writer called Sara Peretsky and I've been reading quite a lot of her books—they're just fun and—

Me: Is that the one who's in the film now?

L: Yes—there's a film. I'm going to see it next week—hopefully.

Me: And what do you like about it?

L: Um—well—its, like, murder—and I like finding out about murder. When I get older I want maybe something to do with law and justice. I kind of like murder books where . . . and she's nice, too, 'cos she's a woman detective and has her ways of finding out about things.

Me: And does she deal with villains?

L: Does she deal with villains—um yes, and she's—er—she came through quite a rough kind of dist . . . in a rough place where she was born, so she knows how to defend herself—knows how to beat people up—

Me: What kind of a rough place?

L: She doesn't quite say, just says a rough part of town. In Chicago or somewhere.

Me: (*Pause*) O.K. Anything else about that?

L: No—but hang on— . . . Not really.

Me: So what else do you like?

L: I read *Pride and Prejudice* quite—well, not very long ago. And I really like that, 'cos its a nice old romantic book—and I like romantic books. It's just nice—'cos you find out about all these characters—there's a lot of sisters and I've got a lot of sisters—so I like to compare it—even though it happened so long ago.

Me: Is it very different—because of that?

L: Yes, it's quite different because of the time—how long ago it was, but you can still compare various things in it, like—they're all so nice to each other in the book—like—it's kind of unbelievable compared—

Me: You think it's not like that now?

L: No. I think they couldn't have been that nice to each other all the time—I think it's just the way it's written.

Me: Mm?

L: Nobody could be that nice to each other all the time really.

Me: You—you're sure of that?

L: Yes—I'm sure! (*laughter*)

Me: Well, how's it compare with you, then?

L: Well, when me and my sisters are all being nice to each other—just doing things with each other—having a good time, really.

Me: Anything more to say about Jane Austen?

L: Well, she's kind of—she's a nice way of quoting things and saying things, and its nice to learn about what happened in that time—in that period, and having to go through this kind of being polite to everybody—and. . . .

Me: You think they're very different? Do you think they were very rich, or were they the same sort of people as we are?

L: Well, it's kind of—you can't really work that one out, 'cos they seem to be very rich—all of the clothes and things—but they're actually not rich compared to some other people in their class—just kind of a way of—but everybody's always trying to—there are so many things you can't do—you can't be seen with certain people—'cos its like being seen talking to the servants outside or whatever . . .

Me: Is that stupid, do you think? or is it different for them than it would be with you?

L: Yes, well—not at all similar to how—well, I mean, Mum doesn't say you can't talk to this person 'cos its bad for your class.

Me: Yes, that is different . . . So, what else, then? What else have you read?

L: Well, I used to like, when I was a little bit younger—I used to like Joan Aiken a lot—and they were just stories of children having adventures—and they were also set quite a long time ago. Well, one, the best one was called *Midnight Is a Place*, and it's just about a little boy—he's lonely and he lives with his guardian, or something and he wishes for a playmate—and he does get one, but it's not what he wanted. It's a little French girl and he starts off really not liking her and finds her a great disappointment 'cos she's kind of stroppy and bad-tempered—and he kind of grows to care for her—they become like brother and sister, and look after each other—and he finds he likes her a lot. And then there's all this stuff going on about all this slave labour going on in the mills—and the little mill children and people being killed 'cos its a big carpet factory and its really dangerous . . .

And Joan Aiken wrote another one—well, she's written quite a few—one of them was called the *Wolves of Willoughby Chase*—which was a kind of a series of books with the same characters and there was this character called Dido—who was just a child heroine—and she was very nice, and she had all these adventures. My favorite one in the series was one—*Night Birds in Nantucket* and it was about how somehow Dido got on to a whaling ship and went right up to America to this little island called Nantucket . . . . What was nice about this was that my Dad—when he was a little boy he used to go to Nantucket for his holiday and he had a house, and because Nantucket is such a tiny island Dad had known all the places on Nantucket—said I've been there and it was such and such here—

Me: But she is an English writer, is she?

L: Yes. This Dido was just a nice little character who went to (?)—having a nasty tutor who was trying to blow the island back to join the mainland, or something—very weird—and she was trying to stop it all and she makes friends on the way who help her and she makes enemies on the way who don't help—she finds out, she discovers all these secrets and stuff . . .

Me: What age is she?

L: Dido? I think she's about ten or eleven—I think. She has great adventures.

Me: Was that—did you read that when you were ten or eleven?

L: Yes, about that. And there's all these other ones that somehow link on to the other stories . . . being a best friend of Dido or something—vaguely connected to Dido.

Me: And that's Joan Aiken?

L: Yes . . . They're just nice—little adventure stories—I don't find them so interesting or exciting anymore—and I really did when I was about ten or eleven or twelve.

Me: Mm . . . What's your latest, then?

L: My latest? Oh I've just started on a Daphne DuMaurier. I can't quite remember what it's called—the tea blowers, or something like that—and that's something to do with glassblowing—a glass blowing family or something—and that's as well—and Dad being a glassblower . . . I think I find I like books where slightly—where I can believe slightly they have something to do with me—maybe 'cos—most of the books I've mentioned are somehow something to do with me, connected to me, if you know what I mean—books I can relate to.

"Books I can relate to": In the role of spectator we create a life of the mind, we read *ourselves*. The range is enormous—the books (as Laurie knows) we can relate to, the stories we tell, the experiences we exchange, the dreams we dream. We learn from them, directly and indirectly, gathering knowledge of the world, past, present, predicted—contemplating what has been and what *might* have been, and inventing the impossible.

Shakespeare's *Midsummer Night's Dream* ends with the celebration of Theseus's wedding to his Amazon bride, Hippolyta. Theseus chooses to see a play prepared by the "hard-handed men that work in Athens here"; but Hippolyta doesn't seem to fancy the idea. Theseus tells her it is all a matter of using your imagination.

> The best in this kind are but shadows, and the worst
> Are no worse, if imagination mend them.

Imagination—the ability to perceive what is conveyed by tacit powers, in a succession of sounds to hear music, as Coleridge reminds us, and in the sounds of words to hear images that reflect our unspoken judgments of reality.

References

Aiken, Joan. (1974). *Midnight is a Place.* Puffin Books.

Appleby, Bruce & Nancy McCracken. (1992). *Gender Issues in the Teaching of English.* Portsmouth, NH: Boynton/Cook

Auden, W. H. (1950). *Collected Shorter Poems, 1930–44.* London: Faber & Faber.

Austen, Jane. (1963). *Pride and Prejudice.* Dent.

Bakhtin, M. M. (1981). *The Dialogic Imagination.* Austin: University of Texas Press.

Batsleer, Janet, Tom Davis, Rebecca O'Rourke & Chris Weedon. (1985), *Re-Writing English: Cultural Politics of Gender and Class.* London and New York: Methuen

Britton, James. (1953). "A Factor Analysis of Poetic Preferences." Technical Information & Documents Unit, Dept. of Scientific & Industrial Research, London.

———. (1952). "An Enquiry into changes of opinion, on the part of adult readers, with regard to certain poems, and the reasons underlying these changes." M.A. in Education, University of London.

———. (1954), "Evidence of Improvement in Poetic Judgement." *British Journal of Psychology, XLV (2)*: 196–208.

———. (1959). "A Study of Responses to Poetry on the Part of Adolescents and Adults." Paper to the Psychology Section, British Association for the Advancement of Science, September. York.

———. (1972). *Language and Learning.* Harmondsworth: Pelican: Rev. ed.

———. (1971). "What's the Use?." *Educational Review, 29* 19 (3):205–219.

———. (1983) "Writing and the Story World." In Barry Kroll & Gordon Wells (Eds.), *Explorations in the Development of Writing* New York: Wiley. (pp. 3–30).

———. (1987). "Call It an Experiment." *English Education*, 19(2): 83–92.

Britton, J., D. Slater, & G. Rogers. (1957). Unpublished report to the Society for Education Through the Arts, November. London.

Britton, James, Tony Burgess, Nancy Martin, Alex McLeod & Harold Rosen. (1975). *The Development of Writing Abilities, 11–18.* New York: Macmillan.

Bruner, Jerome. (1975). "The Ontogenesis of Speech Acts." *Journal of Child Language* (2):1–19.

————. (1986). *Actual Minds, Possible Worlds*. Cambridge, MA: Harvard U. Press.

————. (1988). "Life as Narrative." *Language Arts, 65*(8): 574–83

Bruner, Jerome, A. Jolly & K. Sylva. (1976). *Play*. London: Penguin Books.

Buxton, Charles. (1848). *Memoirs & Correspondence of Sir T. F. Buxton*.

Chukovsky, K. (1989). *From Two to Five*. Berkeley: University of California Press.

Coles, Robert. (1989). *The Call of Stories*. New York: Houghton Mifflin.

DuMaurier, Daphne. (1963). *The Glass Blowers*. Goleance.

Dunne, John. (1593). *Satire III* (extract). See Helen Gardiner (Ed), *The Oxford Book of English Verse* (p. 180). 1972. London: Oxford University Press.

Durst, R., & G. Newell. (1989). "The Uses of Function: James Britton's Category System and Research on Writing." *Review of Educational Research*, 59(4): 375–94

Eliot, George. (1871–2). *Middlemarch*. London: Penguin Classics, 1985.

Eliot, T. S. (1936). *Collected Poems 1909–35*. London: Faber & Faber.

————. (1941). *The Dry Salvages*. London: Faber & Faber.

————. (1942). *The Music of Poetry*. D. W. Harding, *Words into Rhythm* (p. 86). Cambridge: Cambridge University Press.

Eysenck, H. J. (1940). "Some Factors in the Appreciation of Poetry." *Character & Personality*, ix:160–67

Foucault, Michel. (1973). *The Order of Things: An Archaeology of the Human Sciences*, New York: Vintage/Random House

Fuller, Roy. (1942). *The Middle of a War. London: The Hogarth Library*.

Graves, Robert. (1949). *The Common Asphodel*. Hamish Hamilton. London.

Gusdorf, Georges. (1965). *Speaking*. Evanston, IL: Northwestern U. Press.

Harding, D. W. (1937). "The Role of the Onlooker." *Scrutiny, VI*(3):247–58.

————. (1962). "Psychological Processes in the Reading of Fiction." *British Journal of Aesthetics, II*(2): 133–147.

————. (1976). *Words into Rhythm*. London: Cambridge University Press.

Huxley, Aldous. (1932). *Texts and Pretexts*. London: Phoenix Library.

Jakobson, R. (1971). *Selected Writings*, Vol. 2, The Hague: *Mouton*.

Labov, William, & Joshua Waletzky. (1967). "Narrative Analysis: Oral Versions of Personal Experience." in J. Helm (Ed), *Essays on the Verbal & Visual Arts*. Ethnological Journal of America. University of Washington Press.

Langer, Susanne K. (1953). *Feeling and Form*. London: Routledge & Kegan Paul.

Lashley, K. (1961). "The Problem of Serial Order in Behavior." In S. Saporta (Ed), *Psycholinguistics: A Book of Readings*. New York: Holt, Rinehart & Winston.

Leavis, F. R. (1932). *New Bearings in English Poetry*. London: Chatto & Windus.

———. (1944). "Tragedy and the 'Medium'." *Scrutiny*, XII (4)249–60.

———. (1945). "Imagery and Movement." *Scrutiny*, XIII(2): 119–34.

Lewis, N. B. (1934). *The Abolitionist Movement in Sheffield, 1823–33*. Manchester University Press.

Lowry, Malcolm. (1947). *Under the Volcano*. London: Jonathan Cape.

Luria, A. R. & F. Ia Yudovich. (1956). *Speech and the Development of Mental Processes in the Child*. Staples Press: (1971) Penguin.

Luria, A. R. and Vinogradova, O.S. (1959). "The dynamics of Semantic Systems," *British Journal of Psychology, 50*(2): 89–105.

Luria, A. R. (1981). *Language and Cognition*. New York: Wiley.

MacLeish, Archibald. (1935). *Poems*, London: John Lane, The Bodley Head.

MacNeice Louis, (1959). *Collected Poems* London: Faber.

Mill, John Stewart. (1950). In F. R. Leavis, *Mill on Bentham and Coleridge*. (p. 60–62). U.K.: Chatto & Windus.

Moffett, James. (1968). "Drama: What Is Happening." In *Teaching the Universe of Discourse*. (pp. 60–119). New York: Houghton Mifflin.

Morson, Saul. (1991). "Bakhtin and the Present Moment." *The American Scholar*, 60(2):201–22.

Nowottny, Winifred. (1962). *The Language Poets Use*. London: Athlone Press.

Oakeshott, Michael. (1959). *The Voice of Poetry in the Conversation of Mankind*. London: Bowes & Bowes.

Piaget, Jean. (1951). *Play, Dreams and Imitation in Childhood*. London: Heinemann

Polanyi, Michael. (1958). *Personal Knowledge*. London: Routledge & Kegan Paul.

Polanyi, Michael & Harry Prosch. (1975). *Meaning*. Chicago: University of Chicago Press.

Richards, I. A. (1942). *How to Read a Page*. New York: W. W. Norton.

Rose, Mike. (1990). *Lives on the Boundary*. London: Penguin Books.

Rouse, John. (1978). *The Completed Gesture*. Morris Plains, NJ: Skyline Books.

Ryle, John. (1990, January 28). Review of "Seeing Voices," by Oliver Sacks. *Independent on Sunday*.

Sacks, Oliver. (1970). *The Man Who Mistook His Wife for a Hat*. New York: Harper & Row.

Sassoon, Siegfried. (1945). *Siegfried's Journey*. London: Faber & Faber.

Shakespeare, William. (1923). *Complete Works*. New York: Macmillan.

Sitwell, Edith. (1945). *The Song of the Cold*. London: Macmillan.

Stewart, J. I. M. (1949). *Character and Motive in Shakespeare*. London: Longman

Thomas, Dylan. (1952). *Collected Poems*. Dent.

Thomas, Edward. (1951). *Collected Poems*. London: Faber & Faber.

Todorov, Tzvetan. (1977). *The Poetics of Prose* Oxford Blackwell.

Tolstoy, Leo. (1869). *War and Peace*. London: Penguin (translation), 1957.

Volosinov, V. S. (1973) *Marxism and the Philosophy of Language*. Seminar Press.

Vygotsky, L. S. (1962). *Thought and Language*. Cambridge, MA: M.I.T. Press.

———. (1971). *The Psychology of Art*. Cambridge, MA: M.I.T. Press.

———. (1978). *Mind in Society*. Cambridge, MA: Harvard University Press.

Winnicott, Clare. (1977). "Communicating with Children." *Social Work Today*. 8(126): 7–8.

Winnicott, Donald. (1971). *Playing and Reality*. London: Tavistock Publications.

Woolf, Virginia. (1927). *To the Lighthouse*. London: The Hogarth Press.